FRAGILE BUT'

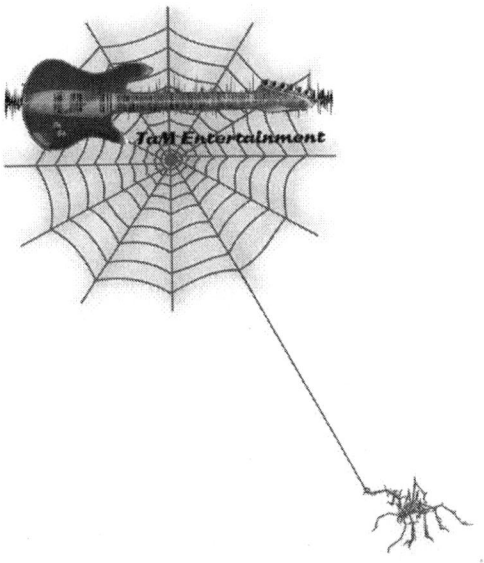

STEVIE ZESUICIDE

A TaM Entertainment publication

FRAGILE BUTTERFLY

STEVIE ZESUICIDE

Fragile Butterfly - Copyright © 2020 by Stevie ZeSuicide

All rights reserved. No part of this book may be reproduced in any form or by any electronic or mechanical means including information storage and retrieval systems, without permission in writing from the author. The only exception is by a reviewer, who may quote short excerpts in a review.

Cover design by Mike Harris

The right of Stephen George Roberts (aka Stevie ZeSuicide) to be identified as author of this work has been asserted in accordance with sections 77 and 78 of the Copyright and Patents Act 1988

Stevie ZeSuicide
Visit my website at www.steviezesuicide.com

Printed in Great Britain

By

TaM Entertainment

First Printing: Apr 2020
TaM Entertainment

ISBN- 9798637766482

INTRODUCTION

So – welcome to the way things can seem.

I so hope that by you reading what I have written about my own experiences you may not feel so alone.

My manager and close friend, Mike Harris, has set up a website – Arize.org.uk – where you can read others' stories and even send in your own for others to read. Maybe through this site you can make contact with other people to talk about anxiety, depression, and other mental issues troubling you – so often caused by immaterial and mundane nonsense.

If you would like printed copies of any of the artwork please get in touch with office@tamentertainment.co.uk who will be more than happy to give you further information.

YOU ARE NOT ALONE

www.arize.org.uk

www.steviezesuicide.com

Arize like daffodils through concrete!

"I have a dream that my four little children will one day live in a nation where they will not be judged by the colour of their skin but by the content of their character."

Martin Luther King

"Our lives begin to end the day we become silent about things that matter."

Martin Luther King

FOREWORD

After the success of his first book – Rock & Roll Chronicles – it was felt that some aspects had been touched on but in no great depth. For that reason Stevie set about to write in more detail about some of the issues that have been a part of his past life.

Over the years Stevie has built up a large collection of poems, some dark in nature, others more lighthearted. These are scattered throughout this book, intermingled with thoughts and comments about how he has been affected by some of the people he has been surrounded by over the years, some beneficial, some not. He also relates some of the anecdotes, not appearing in Rock & Roll Chronicles, concerning famous bands and people he has come into contact with over the years. Add to this all the original drawings and sketches from Stevie's own hand and you have the full package that is – Fragile Butterfly.

So sit back, open the book and read everything with an open mind – some parts you will love, some parts you may not, but all in all this is an insight into Stevie's mind, sometimes carefree, sometimes not.

Judge not lest ye be judged

Matthew 7:1

(See Psycho Vicar chapter)

Mike Harris

(Pity no-one takes any fucking notice!)

One of Stevie's demons

You may have seen this demon in Rock and Roll Chronicles. The thing about demons is that, even after you've dealt with them, they're still there, looking over your shoulder, waiting for you to fail. The moral is – keep on doing what you're doing. Rewards come to those who keep trying – not just to winners. Life is a journey – not a competition - just be the best you can be.

Mike Harris

CONTENTS

Introduction v

Foreword vii

Contents ix

Synopsis Observation 15

Life 18

The Real Stevie ZeSuicide 19

Singapore 27

Little Richard 29

Union Blues 31

I Am an Ant 34

Wrecking Ball 35

God 42

Mother 44

Lordies of Destruction 45

I Am Me 47

Mother's Son 48

Let There be Punk 49

I Am a Flea 53

The 15th, 16th & 17th Century Thugs 54

Crass Encrusted Human 57

Letter from Westminster 58

Arthur's Story 59

Rotting Corpse	61
I Am a Moth	64
Despairing	66
I Have a Dream	68
Village of Peace	69
Black Sabbath	76
Coffin Chronicles	78
Songbird of Life	79
Bay City Rollers	81
Scott Walker	84
Neil Sedaka	86
Personality Disorder, Anxiety, Depression and Alcohol	88
Arize from the Abyss	92
UK Subs (Part 1)	96
Fragile Butterfly	98
The Dead	101
Dragonfly	102
Bruce lee's Defence Technique	105
Jimmy Pursey	107
Vietnam	108
Awards of Excellence	114
Psycho Vicar	115
Dead End Street	119
Classical Punk	121

Death of a Poet	122
Brian May	125
Happy Days	126
Pretty in the City	130
Saturday Screamers	132
I Am an Owl	136
Bob in a Bottle	138
Slade	141
Paparazzi Babes	144
Smell the Art	145
David John Earl	146
I Am a Worm	147
From a Priestess to a Star	148
Hounds of Hell	151
The Great Local Numpty Swindle - Part 1	152
Fuck Pigs of Nonsense	172
The Great Local Numpty Swindle - Part 2	174
Rage of a Vixen	189
Ladybirds and Spiders	190
David Bowie and Marc Bolan	192
My Dead Dad	195
Rock & Roll Gunslingers	197
Live and Let Die	198
The Big 'My Way' Syndrome	200

UK Subs (Part 2)	201
Be a Rainbow	205
Visual Imagery	208
Bob Dylan	210
The Storyteller	211
2nd Class Citizen	212
It's Only Rain	214
Hanoi Rocks	216
I Am a Plant	219
The Ramones	221
Enter The Beatles	224
Into the Void	229
UK Subs (Part 3)	231
Stephen 'Chutch' Drury	233
Enter The Who	234
Mad Albert	240
50 Shades of Death (Pt 1)	241
50 Shades of Death (Pt 2)	243
Canned Heat	245
Witchfinder Generals	246
Lou Reed – Transformer	247
A Soldier's Story	248
A Soldier's Prayer	253
Captain Sensible	254

UK Subs (Part 4)	255
Prelude to an Outlaw	257
Modern Day Outlaw	258
Book of Quotes	263
Special Thanks	271

OPENING THOUGHTS

ABILITY

Ability is only as far as you wish to take it

To shun ability is simply not to be yourself

Your choice… However…

It's not so hard to touch the sky

And not so wrong to try!

Peace of mind is easy

when you ignore the ignorant.

You can defeat oppression by

believing in yourself

SYNOPSIS OBSERVATION

You may find the content of this book a rather disturbing account of unfortunate real life. However I merely wish to pinpoint and highlight those areas set up by numerous flocks of brainless and stubborn, muck-ravaged pinheads.

There is, however a way around this human nightmare, and that is by viewing their many common mannerisms and behavioural patterns as amusing.

Although there is nothing at all funny about most of it – a lot of people are a kind of twisted comedy sketch. Take a look at somewhere like the Leeds Armoury, for instance. A totally accurate example of our warped and twisted evolution, in which we have a huge display of human weaponry – from the Neanderthal's club to our horrendous present day nuclear warheads.

It seems everything in and throughout our history has been designated or built to knock the other side's block off.

The only beauty we behold is within nature and the animals – yet we regularly demolish, persecute and murder them and their environments and habitats for no reason other than money.

Viewing this bloodbath of social existence which we have now made for ourselves, it can only be observed as a living, virtual comedy sketch played out by the insane clowns of destruction. To poke fun at these brainless idiots is the only way I have survived my breakdowns - the "Have you seen my beautiful brand new BMW or Ferrari, or his or her helicopter, or big house complete with oversize pool, false tits and Versace swimwear?"

To co-exist let them all get on in their domestic splendour with no concern for nature what so ever. But don't look down on me…

I'm a Sensitive Boy – a song from UK Subs album 'Diminished Responsibility', written by Charlie Harper – in fact, I don't wanna ever catch them looking at me at all!

It may also help you to remember that… you cannot un-ignorant the ignorant, also, the ignorant are basically unaware of their ignorance.

Blood sports and fox hunters, rabbit killers, and badger murdering scumbags of government don't even realize how mindless they all are in their money-saving cruel misery. They are the soulless membranes who would concrete over our beautiful planet in a second – for cash of course!

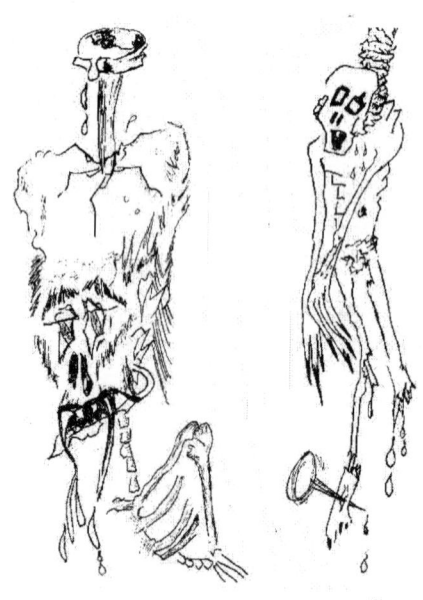

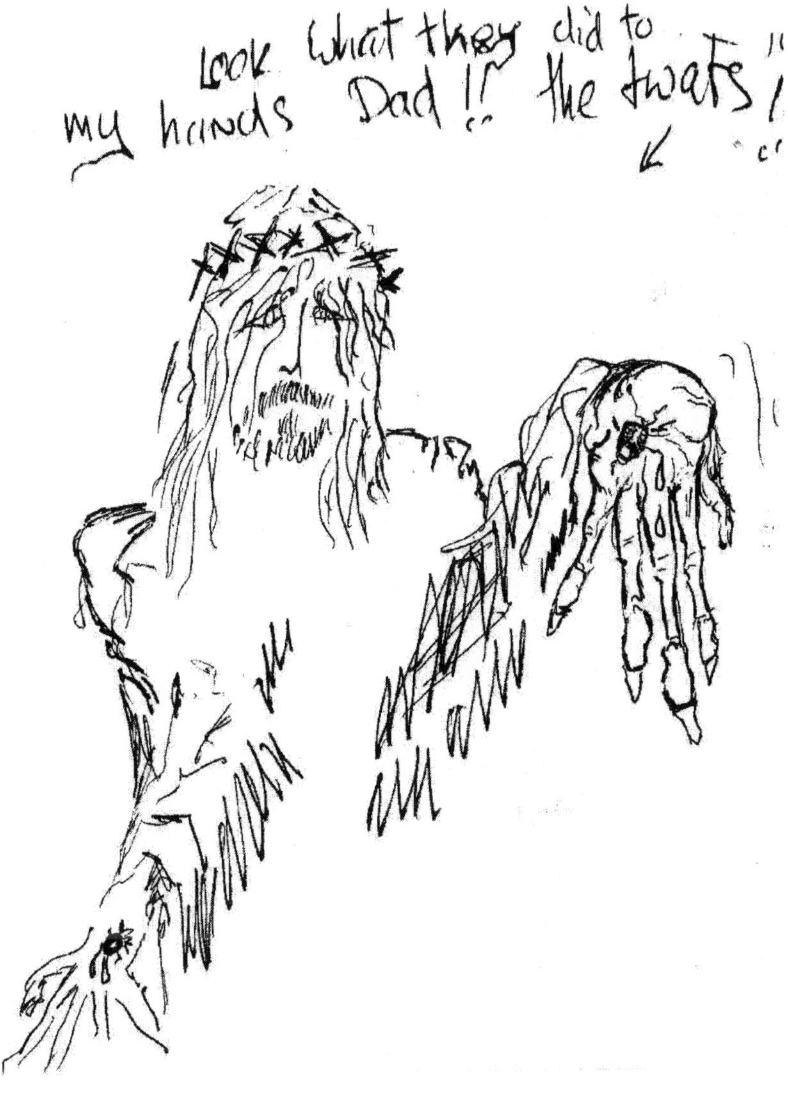
look what they did to
my hands Dad!!
the twats!

LIFE

We are all capable of being good caring people, it only takes a little effort, love and understanding. Manners and respect cost nothing... this is why I am so unimpressed by possessions and wealth. Anyone can have a flash car!! A smile and a kind word costs NOTHING!

Just see the people who look after animals and protect and rescue wildlife.... They, to me, are the true heroes of this life. They have dedication to the things they believe in. Where else in the world would a great rock star like Brian May be allowed to perform his version of our National anthem on the roof of Buckingham Palace? That, my friends, is the freedom and democracy for which so many suffered and died during the wars. We must never forget the freedom they gave us! NEVER EVER!

> *It's easy to forget what greatness really means*
>
> *Yet greatness is the freedom that all our talents need*
>
> *Be the best you can – for it is all you can do*
>
> *Stevie Ze*

There are some nice people out there – you just have to find them, that's all, then life will be so much better – believe me. I am proud to be British. I am proud of our freedom.

THE REAL STEVIE ZESUICIDE

Stevie ZeSuicide is a musician, poet, performer, author, clothes designer and songwriter.

Starting his professional career at only seventeen years old, when he left home and ran away to Singapore with just a rucksack and twenty-six pounds he borrowed off his dad. This was after answering an advert for a professional drummer to play over there in a hotel off the Orchard Road shopping centre – then called The Hotel Malaysia.

The other boys in the band were all mid-twenties and ex-RAF stationed there during their time.

The year is 1971 and he only got the job because nobody else actually applied for it! In fact, at the time, he was considered a little too young by the rest. However when they heard him play it all worked out wonderfully – so off he went.

~ ~ ~

Stevie continues: We played on a standard Musician's Union approved contract of six nights a week, four hours a night.

Now, that all seems a long time but as well as that, the venue would also insist you played on Sundays, the one day off, as a separate gig, just like the way my dad's band played at Caesars Palace. So actually they got you to play on an otherwise illegal seven day week – or 'six nights and every Sunday' as this was known in MU terms.

This was my musical schooling. Blisters on fingers and a total education in survival and musicianship. Most of all experience you just couldn't pay for – so why stay at home when you can practice live on stage and get paid for it?!

On returning to Britain I joined one or two covers bands before launching onto the cabaret circuit. I was often in bother as I had learned showmanship – how to juggle the sticks and be a character like my idols, Gene Kruper and fabulous drum genius, Buddy Rich – then later after seeing The Who and watching the mighty Keith Moon work, my reputation as a rebel grew. Getting signed to top agents like McCloud Holden was a smart move.

My job was to back big artists coming over from America… cabaret and show venues were rife in those days with 'Talk of the Town', 'Caesars Palace', of course, 'Batley Variety Club', 'The Futurist' and 'Spa' in Scarborough, 'Blackpool Winter Gardens' and many, many more.

Those US acts didn't always have the budget to bring a whole band over so agents and managers like Tony French would supply whatever musicians were needed to perform each particular show… and everybody always needed a drummer!

I was part of a wonderful team of players. Being the drummer I ended up setting all the tempo's and counting everyone in. During this time I toured on drums behind American legends such as James and Bobby Purify, The Drifters, Johnny Johnson and the Bandwagon, Jimmy Ruffin, Little Richard – and Britain's own rock and roll star, the great Billy Fury.

During my first show with James and Bobby Purify, Jimmy counted in their sixties hit 'I'm your Puppet', way too fast. After the show I felt I had to tell him – a pretty brave thing for a nineteen year old to say to a soul legend. He listened, however, and said,

"Okay then, Stevie boy, you count it in." And from that day I did. The same happened with The Drifters.

Playing at the correct tempo, we achieved a much warmer soulful sound – plus it was then more like the record – the audience loved it! I was perfecting my art and the work was pouring in.

When I started with Billy Fury I was struck by his similarity to Elvis and suggested to him that I start the show with a massive drum rhythm, just like Elvis' drummer Ronnie Tutt would always do to start their Vegas shows. Over this he would be introduced… "Ladies and gentlemen… the one and only Billy Fury!" and he would walk on in his gold lamé suit as the band started. This was so effective and worked a treat, projecting his brilliant stage presence to the max, and creating such exciting drama for a live show. He was pleased with it and so were his fans.

When Billy Fury passed away on 28th Jan 1983 I was devastated.

I always wanted a Gene Vincent tour but missed out by a few weeks – I think it was a band called Sounds Incorporated who got that one, the lucky devils, as that one also involved a high profile TV show – still used to this day for his stunning performance of Be Bop a Lula. Being a rocker myself I eventually got my TV spot with Little Richard – and what an experience, as you can read later in this book.

My other great hero to work with was Jimmy Ruffin, his hit of 'What becomes of the Broken-Hearted?' – still one of my all-time favourite records – and playing it live behind the man himself was pure job perfection!

Time progressed into Punk and I was straight there, not only joining UK Subs, but recording with The Exploited on their 'Troops of Tomorrow' album, and playing live on stage with The Damned.

Now with Punk I was in my real element – I honestly feel I was born a punk. When I was a young lad, even at junior school, I so hated authority and stupid rules! To me the teachers were like thick bullies, looking and talking total crap, and next to The Beatles and Bob Dylan they meant nothing and indeed they were nothing. The way they treated us in those days – like we were just shite!

Punk rock gave me a reason to live. Punk rock gave me a freedom to express myself far beyond the blinkered muso's and, for me, what better reason to perform?

I joined York punk band 'Cyanide' first, then moved on to UK Subs but I still did other projects alongside this such as recording with The Exploited and playing live with The Damned.

Yet, although all the tours with UK Subs were so very special, doing Top of the Pops with Charlie, Nick and Alvin were amongst the BEST days of my career. I am so proud of those albums and singles, and the tours were just awesome!

Then suddenly and out of the blue I had to deal with a lot of parasitic twats, the posh came in to take our money or attempt to burn us to death. Even when I went on to work backstage on films later on, the cocaine-fuelled public school spoilt gang and creepy snobs would talk down to me. Who, or what the hell do these creatures think they are? I would ask myself. But I learned my lessons well – nobody ever got away with it twice… and never will!

I was then asked by director Simon West to appear in a Sony Mini Hi-Fi advert for the American TV channel MTV. Simon had just finished filming the Lara Croft, Tomb Raider movies with Angelina Jolie. I was so pleased when he asked me and the ad was fun. I then just missed out on a 'Sure' antiperspirant ad by a single day. I received a message "Can I get home quick?" but, in those days before mobile phones I missed out to a model who knew nothing about playing drums and a chick who'd probably never even seen a saxophone! Very frustrating – but that's show biz!

However, Simon Cowell saw the Sony ad and booked me to play drums behind his singer Sinitta on her videos, which included, 'I don't Believe in Miracles', which was previously a successful song by sixties band The Zombies.

Moving into film:

I invented a cheeky little number for myself by suggesting to producer Jacquie Byford that all these huge stars she was filming music videos for needed a personal assistant – a kind of pink-haired punk butler with personality to match… solely to look after them and their dressing rooms, or whatever you keep them in.

She answered, "You mean you?" and I got the job. My first film gig was with Elton John. I then proceeded to work with Diana Ross, Tina Turner, The Rolling Stones, KISS, AC/DC, Freddie Mercury, Spandau Ballet, Iggy Pop, Queen and many more. Although only a glorified tea boy, in their dressing rooms and on set it was a priceless education, I couldn't have wished for more. This helped immensely towards the next, and rather unexpected, stage of my career as a vocalist, frontman guitarist and songwriter. I mean, to stand next to performers like Mick Jagger, Tina Turner or Diana Ross observing how they work to the camera was absolutely priceless to me – plus they were also extremely encouraging and kind.

While working with The Stones I was asked by their PR man what it meant to me as a punk to be working with them. I told him it was like being with five uncles who you've never met before but who you've known all your life. He seemed to like that answer and wrote it down – but it's true and it was ever so exciting!

Shortly after this I was put into a studio to record my own songs and sing them – which I did gladly. I was working closely with David Bowie's legendary bassist Trevor Bolder – who was producing and playing various guitars. Together we came up with two albums worth of material – all my own original songs together with a collection of videos which I directed and produced myself.

You can read about this time, and more, in Stevie ZeSuicide's earlier book 'Rock & Roll Chronicles' outlining his extraordinary life. Available from Amazon books as paperback or eBook for Kindle.

Mike Harris

SINGAPORE

"I felt trapped on a suburban landslide

of nothingness, waiting to be nailed into

place with the rest of them.

I just had to leave!

Stevie Ze

Well, as you've already read by now, at seventeen I left home to live and work in Singapore playing drums in a hotel down there on Orchard Road called The Malaysia. The year is 1971 and I stayed about a year or so.

My agent in Singapore was a certain Michael Tan, a wonderful man of great integrity. Michael had a warehouse and studio jammed full of instruments, mainly guitars and basses dating from as early as the fifties up to the present day.

I was amazed at the skills of my Chinese, Indian and Pakistani friends, all around my age, who seemed to have an ability to pick up an instrument and play it at the drop of a hat.

What hours of pleasure and fun we all had… I would be playing in the hotel at night then spending nearly every day with my friends at the warehouse, where I started to learn my T Rex! We were all listening to Led Zeppelin and Deep Purple at the time – no easy task to play, yet no problem for my Singapore pals. We must have formed two or three different bands a week between us!

There was a Malaysian guy who just played all day, every day, then all night at his hotel The Ming Court. He specialised so superbly in all that really fast Les Paul jazz stuff. Jazz solos you just wouldn't believe were possible. Our guitarist Dave Smith was so impressed by what he saw, he jokingly once said, "Christ, can't you play any faster?" to which he demonstrated his technique even faster than he was already playing. Dave added, "I was only joking." This hadn't translated properly and he played even faster, with seemingly no effort!

I really miss my friends over there. They were all so great and when there was something on guitar I couldn't handle during our jamming sessions, I would simple jump on to the drums, "Easy peasy," then of course, at night it was back to the hotel to play 'til dawn.

During the night in Singapore all the car parks by day would transform into beautiful food and drink stalls known as Makan (I hope I've spelt that right.) After the shows I would immediately zoom down there to meet up with the others and hang out, taste the food – the wonderful food cooked in the woks on the spot… drink the fresh cool fruit drinks blended with ice in giant glasses, skins, pips and all – this was heaven to me. And we would naturally chat 'til dawn about our favourite artists. People would bring down their guitars and instruments and we'd sing and play until the sun came up!

I remember one of my close friends, James 'Jimi' Appoduria Chua, had a Gibson 335 like BB King and we even had someone with a sitar. And the smells – the absolutely wonderful range of different aromas from the food still linger with me to this day!

Great company! Great food! Loyal friendships and first class hospitality! Singapore is my beautiful second home. Maybe even, if the truth is known, my first home.

LITTLE RICHARD

I was asked by Mike Laycock, chief editor at The Press, in York, just how I could have forgotten playing drums behind the legend that is rock and roll star Little Richard on a TV show during a tour I was on in early seventy-one/seventy-two. The fact is I was in Germany with a working band when a call came through to our hotel at a ludicrous time in the morning – no mobiles or computers in those days, remember.

It was our manager back in England, Tony French, to inform us we were booked to back another American artist on a live TV show, just one number, the artist was Little Richard and the TV studio was nearby, plus it was good extra money. So off we went, fairly bleary-eyed first thing in the morning.

On arrival we got set up nice and early. At the front of the stage was this black grand piano, complete with open lid and gold candelabra, like Liberace or somebody would have, yet the piano was really battered and scratched up, like a demon had attacked it! I was so impressed as this was Little Richard's very own piano.

In those days we never even thought of a rehearsal. Just do it. No nerves, no hesitation. The song we were to do was 'I Hear You Knockin' But You Can't Come In' a simple 12-bar in A which starts off with the drums. Easy peasy! So we awaited our star's arrival.

As he arrived we were told to stand by for orders. The TV show's director, who spoke in German, would announce, "Lights, cameras" then point to me as my cue, then, "Action." And drums would start.

We waited a couple of hours until our call came to be on stage, then it was time. "Lights, cameras," the finger pointed, "Action." I started the big drum intro which I adored playing with energy and mentalness – so I really went for it! Little Richard clocked my performance and was clearly pleased with his fellow lunatic on drums.

After the performance he bowed to the audience and left the stage. As he passed me he smiled and winked at me, as if to say, "That showed 'em, son." Another precious moment in my life I'll never forget.

To this day people ask me what he was like to which I can only reply, I have absolutely no idea as I never met him!"

We simply packed our gear back in the van and set off to our next gig... after being paid, of course!

UNION BLUES

Expelled by a duffle coat clad jazz goon. Now let's not forget the working men's club and pub tribute act, living abortion element.

All the plumbers, bricklayers, electrical and gas pipe qualified nine to fivers who unashamedly have put so many full time musicians out of work with their amateur karaoke-backing track machines – eliminating live players in order to fill their greedy amateur pockets with extra swag!

These berks are nothing like the real thing, and never can be as they have no brains or original show biz talent of their own. In fact you may as well watch a garden slug. Yet if we were to take their jobs off *them* they would be the first creeps crying in their beers before running off to their unions for help.

The mighty Musicians Union, however, do absolutely nothing to protect us from all these parasitic hopefuls who, for whatever reason, couldn't do music properly in earlier years, probably because they were too frightened, too married to their hapless boilers, too mortgaged, so scared of a day or two off precious work, too busy changing nappies, or perhaps too simple to take a risk.

And let's not forget the most probable reason – too talentless!

Now, "Musicians Union" – what a joke! Yet they collect subscriptions from all their members… for what, I do not know.

I was a proud member for all of my many years during my days of Top of the Pops and world tours, always keeping up with my membership subscriptions – until I fell upon some hard times whilst putting Stevie ZeSuicide together, what with recording albums and producing my own videos, it was hard.

I was expelled, viciously and without remorse, by the new MU secretary for York after the lovely Alf Field passed away. I had fallen behind with my subs to the tune of twenty pounds. I was subsequently thrown out within an hour of the arrival at my door by the new secretary, who was rather insulting to say the least, and who clearly did not like or respect punk rock, or indeed any of the "noisy beggars" as he presented me with an ultimatum – "Pay up by six pm or get out!"

The late Alf Field, the original secretary was a pioneer and a total supporter of original creativity, and understood how hard it can be to survive professionally for musical artists of all types. Now he had gone and I was faced with this duffle coat clad jazz goon, sitting in my own home surrounded by my gold discs, telling me, "The trouble with you lot is…"

My dad, the late George Roberts, a true professional pianist (not a local dabbler) had worked at Caesars Palace, Talk of the Town, live TV shows with the likes of Tom Jones and Lulu. In retirement as my family came back to York he continued to work, playing at Batley Variety Club, The Futurist in Scarborough and Cottingham Country Club, amongst others – now all such wonderful venues sadly closed.

My dad had been a lifelong member, even receiving a MU pension, I had always been a member on his advice, yet this jazz goon, with no capability of understanding anything about my musical background arrived at my door and gave me an hour to pay up or be thrown out.

I found it so upsetting! My dad wanted to pay it for me but I wouldn't let him as any belief I had once had in supporting this supposedly protective organisation had been destroyed.

Remember that many of the most original artists out there have been broke and in need of help – not deserving a pounding into depression like this power mad bully did to me!

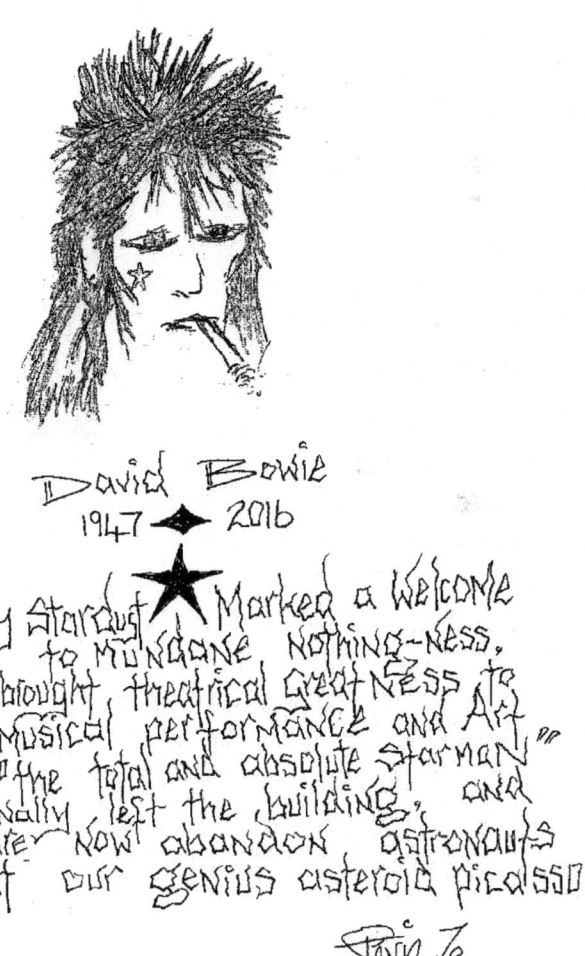

I AM AN ANT

My God... I am an ant
no need to rave or rant
and if I get in your pants,
you'll jump & scream & dance,
with beauty so enhanced
yet so tiny
at a glance,
& My Armys
will advance
this Earth
that we
inchant
we have
to take
our chance,... so we often sing & dance
we carry leaves so heavy
to build our tunnels many
I like my sugar rich, and
Millipede with chias just
like yours, snake teas which stengthens
all my needs, designed to work so hard
we can brighten up your yard
I have great legs & jaws
with a charm you can't ignore
I'm just a little Ant
please love me if you can!!

WRECKING BALL

Traipsing around record labels with my new-found music, I found doors slammed in my face, secretary's almighty self-importance fired straight at me in the form of their extreme ignorant rudeness – the like of which I had never been subjected to, of course, while selling records and doing Top of the Pops, in fact I was in no way equipped to take any of it!

However, at one of my stops – Polygram – I was greeted with a very positive reaction to my work and spent a couple of genuinely nice hours going through my songs. The chap's name was Peter something or other, I can't remember, but he was very pleased with what he heard.

He explained to me how he had once made a huge mistake in turning down singer Eddi Reader with her song 'Perfect' – a later massive Number One hit for Fairground Attraction! He said he didn't want to make the same mistake again. We got on well, and he proceeded to phone my then manager and inform him of all this, with talk of studio time and a single…

Then, to my horror, on the way out there sat a 'wrecking ball' – who I'm calling Crispy Lip of York, a well-known user and jumper of bandwagons. "What are *you* doing here?" he patronisingly snapped, as if I had absolutely no right being in a posh gaff like Polygram.

I replied, "I have to be somewhere," and quietly and politely walked away. Crispy Lip had followed me like a parasitic tick after I had joined 'Cyanide' and 'UK Subs' but I was stupid enough to take this two-faced creep to Top of the Pops with us, and introduced him to everyone he wanted to meet, like publishers, etc.

Crispy Lip was shocked and put out because it was him who told me I could never play a guitar or write a song… and he was now next in to see Peter Thingy. On my return home, feeling really good about the future, I received a rather disturbing call from my manager to say that all had gone terribly wrong. How could this happen? I had simply had my character assassinated just like a pink-haired J F Kennedy by the Crispy Lip wrecking Ball. Bang! Out to destroy whatever he is not involved in.

> *"Well once a very great man said*
>
> *That some people rob you with a fountain pen*
>
> *Don't take too long to find out*
>
> *Just what he's talking about."*
>
> *Bob Dylan*

What followed were several soul-destroying train trips down to London only to face numerous humiliating turn-downs, often without even listening to either me or my music. Whilst back in London I decided to visit some of my old haunts where I had lived once so happily in Chelsea, SW3. It was a terrible time, but I was determined – if not a little frustratingly impatient!

I wandered around in a punch drunk daze at the horrible-ness of people who were once all over me yet now scorn me. At this stage in my life I was, for the first time since leaving school, a musical outcast. I wandered alone, along familiar streets of my beloved Chelsea where I was so happy before moving to York and letting in the amateur chancers who had put me out of business – and who I should never have met!

> *"Never regret being a good person to the wrong people,*
>
> *Your behaviour says everything about you.*
>
> *And their behaviour says everything about them."*
>
> Bruce Lee

I visited the famous Kings Head and Eight Bells, in Cheyne Walk, where The Rolling Stones used to hold a lot of their meetings during the sixties, when Brian Jones was still alive. And, indeed, it was where I had had my final drink with Def Leppard guitarist Steve Clark on the very day he died. (More on this in my first book 'Rock & Roll Chronicles in the 'Sheffield Steel' chapter.)

For years when I lived there I visited Battersea Park on a daily basis to walk my doggie, Trudie. I used to often meet a nice chap called Cliff Adams whilst he was walking his lovely collie dog, Whistler. We talked at great length about all sorts of topics, including music. Weeks passed by then one evening he suddenly appeared on a TV show, as requested by a loyal fan.

Who was this nice man who lived in the next street to me in Chelsea? When I saw him on TV I realised he was non-other than broadcaster and musical composer Cliff Adams and the Adams Singers – who carried a well-known Radio Two show called 'Sing Something Simple' for many, many years. It went out at tea time every Sunday and was a relaxing tonic to millions of listeners, including my Grandad – a regular listener over a ham salad and a peaceful evening.

He would always advise me "Get yourself a jingle, the money's in advertising jingles." He told me the simple story of the mashed potato ads, when he was asked to write a simple jingle about aliens trying to make mash! He told me he submitted several versions which kept coming back to be shortened. The final accepted, and almost sarcastically short, version was "For mash get Smash." One bar long, but they screamed their approval. The jingle was used in several different languages across the globe. "And that can buy a house for you, boy," he insisted, "Get yourself a jingle." Sound advice from the lovely Cliff Adams.

I went to see my old basement garden flat at 106 Oakley Street, Chelsea, SW3 – it hadn't changed but I wondered why I had ever left, and why, for God's sake, to York and not to Leighton Buzzard.

In Oakley Street, one of my all-time heroes, Georgie Best lived at number 87, and at the bottom of my garden lived Bill Travers of the movie 'Born Free', who I would often chat to on a sunny day. An extremely polite and gentle person. In fact the whole of Chelsea was a hive of activity in art, dance, drama, fashion and music. Wonderful looking people – so expressive and creative.

By now I was feeling a bit crumpled and rather sad at the now big hole that was once my beloved career. So there I was with all my songs and poems, my hair, my nail polish and return ticket back to York, back to God-forsaken Yorkshire.

Even more wonderfully grim nothingness. I knew there was nothing there for a seriously original artist. So, before I went home, I decided to walk back to Kings Cross Station via Cheyne Walk. There was Rolling Stones' Keith Richard's old house at Number 3, and drummer Charlie Watts' flat a bit further down. Thinking back, I recalled always putting the bins out on a Wednesday evening before tea. One evening a very dapper gentleman in a pin stripe suit said, "Hello," as he passed. As I looked up, to my joy, I realised it was Charlie, who had recognised me from the video I had worked on for 'One Hit to the Body.' (See

Rock & Roll Chronicles). I answered, "Hi, have a nice evening," and Charlie walked on, grey haired, with a slight bald patch at the back. The man in one of the top jobs in Rock & Roll, who'd been there all my life. He'd been to Waitrose, and carried two carrier bags of wine and bits. Every inch a rock legend but, above all, a totally well-mannered and respectful gentleman. That meant so much to me.

Dreaming away, I proceeded until I reached the middle of Cheyne Walk where I had an obscure, and probably desperate, idea. This was the palatial home of John Paul Getty – well known as a recluse, but also for putting the odd fortune behind true artists such as me…

I think it was around this time that my mental health had started to deteriorate and, hurtling towards 'victim status', I decided the best bet was to scale the wall in order to present him with my work – poems and music – and maybe, just maybe, he will invest in me with some sponsorship for Stevie ZeSuicide.

The wall was a breeze – being an athletic drummer had left me fit as a fiddle so up went. After all, Sir Robert Falcon Scott had only lived around the corner of Oakley Street, and he had found his way to the South Pole – although he never came back, and his mate Oates wandered off to get lost. How grim. Yet that's British spirit for you!

Anyhow, there I was at the summit of the Getty wall looking over, where I noticed several security cameras following my progress. In my naivety I started waving at them, thinking that he can see me now! Then I suddenly heard sirens blaring and I looked down in the street to see several police cars and a police van pulling up with screeching tyres, noisily backed up by an armed response team shouting, "COME DOWN NOW!" at me through a megaphone. I jumped straight down – not into the street, but into the yard, where I was met by a rather irate Filipino maid who proceeded to beat me with a sweeping brush. The police entered and ordered her to stop!

Suddenly there was silence, but they didn't handcuff me, instead asked what the Hell I thought I was playing at, with a gun pointing at my nostrils. I explained about my art and was immediately offered a deal – not with Getty, sadly, but from the cops. They told me that if I promised to get on the train and go far away back to York they would not arrest me. In fact that insisted on driving me to Kings Cross and seeing me safely onto the next train.

I happily agreed to this, my mission in tatters, rather like Scott of the Antarctic. As I was getting into the police car I was still being shouted at by the Filipino maid to the point where I couldn't resist calling back to her, "Any chance of a sandwich for the journey, doll?" She responded rather badly, getting even more ballistic, and beat me around the head with her broom again before the police drove me away.

They stayed with me on the station until I was safely on board and the train was moving off, still with my almost finished half bottle of whisky, and as I travelled back to York I added a bottle of British Rail wine.

Back at home I looked back over my busy day and as I thought how lucky I was to be alive, I would start to doubt the reason for my existence at all! It's hard to live with rejection, especially from those who you thought were one your friends…

But I would fight back and return with my music, art and design – whatever they've said or done to hurt me, and THAT is THAT!

"Water is not hard
But it can cut through
Rock and steel
Because of its
PERSISTANCE!"

Stevie Ze

You must never let others put you off –
no matter how hard they try.

"Beware the Wrecking Ball."

"Everyone you meet is
fighting a battle
you know nothing about
be kind… always."

Robin Williams

GOD

God is hollow
God is blind
God is nothing
And so unkind

God is the Reaper
Bent and twisted
God is a war zone
And we are enlisted

God is treason
God is hate
God is people
False and fake

God is no-one
Who exists

Yet we're the blisters

On his evil fists

God is Beatles

God is Dylan

His faith is a villain

Obsessed with killing

"Sometimes it's not the artist I don't like – it's the people who like that artist." Stevie Ze

MOTHER

Mother

content & happy
she filled my days
with fun & laughter
in every way

giving joy & love
& so much more
my wonderful mum
who I adore

you'll never leave us
all alone, ... for you
I'd give up all I own

I will love you
till the day I die
when again we'll meet
up in the sky

I long to be
beside you now
your far away
yet close somehow

I hope your there
the day I die
to walk together
up to the sky

LORDIES OF DESTRUCTION

This book is dedicated to all those who have been cheated and lied to, and generally torn into pieces by the soulless and insensitive who care about nothing or no-one except themselves.

The greedy music thief and overambitious parasitic two-faced control freaks who try to change you into what *they* think you should be like!

The money, money mad power clan treading down on anyone or anything which may stand in the way of filling up their greedy bottomless pockets with gold.

From the property developer chopping down a simple, harmless tree which was home to so many sparrows or other birds, to the amateur bozo tribute singers putting so many real musicians out of work with their cheap cretinous backing tapes.

Yes, these are the clueless, zero-talent blood suckers who feed off the misery of so many others without a single thought for ART! Usually existing within the safety of a herd of sheep-minded wildebeest and criticising the world from within their hapless flock.

These septic creatures can grind you down into their own inevitable blandness- thus crushing any dreams or thoughts you may have of any creative originality, or indeed a better life style.

These Lordies of Destruction are known commonly as…

Human Beings!

Riding roughshod over our precious rain forests and beautiful wildlife until there's nothing left. When all the time this Earth is not the sole property of human beings alone… but a loving home to all the wonderful living creatures of all shapes and sizes who were not only born here, and with whom we should all be proud to share it with, and many of whom are descended from generations living here long before we were.

A superb example of Christian hypocrisy is the fact that you may enter a church only if dressed posh enough for the upper middle classes, yet none of our so-called God's creatures are allowed in! If you've ever tried turning up at a christening or a wedding with a llama, pet frog or a donkey you would be turfed out for sure.

So, from the person who derives some kind of sadistic pleasure from shooting a defenceless animal dead… to the child molester, the serial killer, the burglar, the street thug… from politically induced mass murder to cowardly blood sports and animal cruelty – these people are all only on step away from each other in both their thoughts and their behavioural patterns of activity.

How the hell do we co-exist with all this without the most caring and rationally-minded members of our society breaking down in some way?

Be original… be yourself

And yet, use your influences in such a positive way

That you can make them your own

And find that inner self worth.

Stevie Ze

I AM ME

Tough as glass

Yet easily shattered

Broken in two

By things that matter

Yet, if I break

Make no mistake

For whist I weep

I may cut you deep

With words alone

And without your violence

I strive to vent

My pending vengeance

MOTHER'S SON

Mother's son

the sun shines down
upon an urban street,
full of Beer, Gin & Gasoline,..
see the sanitized smiles,
& the wives
Who keeps the white shirts clean,..
& clever Mr Big
buys a smart new suit,
Just to be the boss's No 1,
claims he was a punk,
but he's just another,
Mother's son,..

LET THERE BE PUNK

The beginning of time

After years on the road I had ended up in the city of York for some bizarre reason unexplained to everyone... yet I was optimistic about my music and my future.

The first person to latch onto punk in York was my good old friend and colleague in the bands, our tour manager, and now award-winning photographer Stephen James Drury – known to his friends as 'Chutch'.

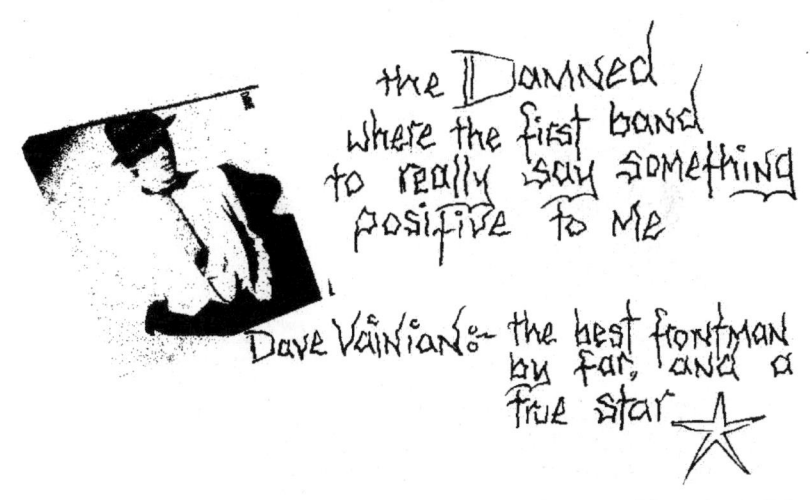

the Damned where the first band to really say something positive to me

Dave Vainian's- the best frontman by far, and a true star

I remember we were doing a gig somewhere with a horrible and frighteningly amateur rock as Plasticene Mummy and Daddy's boys called... What was their name??? Anyway, by this time Chutch and I were both bored to tears with all this "Daren't gig past Selby' bollocks. A rebellion was *so* needed – a revolution to get rid of all the baldy stale crap that was by now clogging up the airwaves and preventing any bright new talent from getting through!

We heard The Damned's 'New Rose,' I think it was, and my life was transformed in an instant. "That's it, Chutch, I'm off to join a REAL band and not a flock of blind sheep smelling each other's bottoms for direction." He agreed and began working, almost immediately, with top sound man, engineer Dave Leaper – York's all-time music guru and punk entrepreneur par excellent. He also managed a brand new fresh punk band 'Cyanide'. On my drums I joined the band shortly afterwards.

GREAT DAYS!

Now Cyanide consisted of Dave 'Zef' Stewart on lead guitar, Dave 'Jock' Marsden on bass, and fabulously entertaining and flamboyant front man with so much stage presence, and song-writing genius, Bob DeFries, and, of course… ME… (above l to r - me, Zef, Bob and Paul Ash)

I played on three Cyanide singles – 'Your Old Man', 'The Mess I Am', and Zef's fantastic composition 'Fireball'. They are all great songs – but then all Bob's and Zef's songs were great – fabulously honest protests of real life personified… and produced by the wonderful Dave Leaper, our manager and all round great bloke, known as 'Dad,' by Bob and the band.

The scene was set and this team was York punk at its best – there we were in the middle of it all.

Cyanide's brilliant, one and only album entitled 'Cyanide' still sells and is a punk collectors' piece to this day. Shortly after its release I joined the band on drums, but to my disappointment a new bass player was needed when Jock decided to leave the band to marry his long-time girlfriend Carol and settle down. So bassist Paul Ash was bought in to replace him for a forthcoming tour set up by manager Dave 'Dad' Leaper. This tour was special as we would be the opening act for the already successful UK Subs, who were already proudly sporting two top twenty albums, 'Another kind of Blues', and 'Brand New Age.'

Just prior to all this life-changing mayhem I remember playing in a 'working mens' club' trio on my drums and, although it was regular and quite an experience, I was really feeling extremely bored and distraught – but I needed to make a living so there I was.

Then, one night, Chutch turned up to watch me play. He'd been on tour by now with UK Subs and The Ramones – the mighty Ramones! He was dressed in a black suit, black tie and white shirt, sporting a cool pair of shades. A head to foot professional, creating a powerful image of punk's rock and roll energy. It was then that I realized just what a great time it was for brand new styles and fashion. I soon discovered Vivian Westwood's collection with her jackets and shirts, and her use of zips, bondage straps and Doc Martins.

My stage was set!

Then it came! The Sex Pistols – both 'Anarchy in the UK' and 'God Save the Queen' singles, and despite both making Number One in the charts, their name was blanked out of the billboards due to total media fear!

MUSICAL EXCELLENCE!

The revolution had started. My future was sealed and little did I know that soon I would be living in Kings Road, Chelsea, SW3 after joining the fabulous UK Subs when original drummer Pete Davis left.

We toured the world extensively at the top of our game – producing more top twenty albums, appearing on Top of the Pops and staying in the finest hotels like punk kings! Life was full on! We had everything… top rock and roll, chaos, anarchy, and, as Stevie Ze now – 'the Destruction of Boredom!'

> *I definitely like being a star –*
>
> *it's the only thing I do that doesn't bore me*
>
> David Bowie

But Cyanide were certainly the boys to be with – well ahead of their time. When Cyanide singer Bob DeFries sadly passed away it cast such a dark shadow over so many. And shortly before this, original bass player Jock was tragically killed in a car accident, along with his wife Carol and baby daughter. This had a profound effect on everyone, but especially Bob, who I felt never got over it.

"May your God bless them all"

I AM A FLEA

My God

I am a flea
+ you can't see me wee
I am so very small
so I jump instead of crawl

I have a little dog
who's blood will fill my gob
+ feed me all my life
so I have no need for flight

I may be just a flea
but at least I know I'm me
my life is all I've got
+ I love my life a lot

THE 15ᵀᴴ, 16ᵀᴴ & 17ᵀᴴ CENTURY THUGS

But where are they now?

I have a theory about those who carried out the most horrific acts of barbarism against their fellow human beings during the 15th, 16th and 17th centuries – especially during the terrifyingly cruel reign of Henry VIII.

People were sawn in half while still alive, tortured beyond belief, tongues cut out, ears hacked off, hung up to die in chains, boiled alive in water or oil, made to sit on red hot seats whilst strips of flesh were torn from their bodies with red hot pliers.

Young girls and women were slowly drowned or burnt at the stake for 'maybe' being a witch, by perverted church men who, no doubt, possessed huge erections whilst carrying out their barbaric, murderous jollities of extreme sexual pleasure –

"Witchfinder the General"

and all in the name of God, or Jesus, and all legal under the instructions of the hideously spoilt and evil king.

However… these mindless jobsworths of sheer unimaginable cruelty and suffering did not just die out, or suddenly become extinct. No! In fact these murderous control freaks are still around us today, and unfortunately with us on a daily basis. Of course, they now have to work in different professions as sadistic barbarism and torture are no longer a legal career move!!

Beware, my beautifuls, you can easily find the same mentality hiding in disguise as policemen, MP's, councillors, traffic wardens, supermarket management, TV chefs, pub landlords and their thug bouncers, vicars and priests – or whatever psycho bully employment they choose.

You name it… you'll always find ONE!

So next time you are pushed, bossed around or bullied at school or in the workplace, or anywhere for that matter, just think – you may be face to face with a next generation medieval psycho! BEWARE parish councillors (witchfinder generals), pre-judgemental Christian shit-stirrers and other religious, trouble-causing NUTTERS!

Bishops secretly in ladies underwear, and vibrating epileptic monks, your teachers, your managers and all the numerous other arse-wiping servants of our planet's blatant ignorant!

"Take away their power, ignore them all

Be strong with Pride, be proud, be happy, you are beautiful

Each one of us is a rainbow of love

Not a subject of hate"

Stevie Ze

CRASS ENCRUSTED HUMAN

And how their nastyness
makes me strong
within the crazyness
of constant wrong..

let them live in
their bubble of hate
and petty vendettas
they all create..

for None could exist
without some trouble!
to gossip about
or a drama to cuddle,.

within their huddle
of sheep mentality
devouring burgers
of bland morality..

I hope they cry, inside their tombs,..
of wretched crass encrusted gloom

LETTER FROM WESTMINSTER

Westminster through a medium

Hello

I am Adolf Hitler, and I want you all to know that I am still with you... through your Government, your church, the vicars, Parish Councils, Residents Associations and, of course, our wonderful police force!

My old friend Mussolini helps by running our golf clubs' hierarchy, local MP's, Rotary Clubs, and general elitist small village muck. Whilst little Napoleon, bless him, has all the Working Mens' Club Committee members and runs the Musicians' Union.

So, with all my brand new little helpers, just vote with any political party whatsoever and I will once again be in power – be it only in spirit and influence.

Sincerely, always yours, I promise – honest

Adolf

ARTHUR'S STORY

If we can just accept people for what they are and can view the funny side of their characters it would make life so much more amusing and happy. I really wish we were all more sympathetic towards each other's little ways

An elderly gentleman called Arthur lived next door to my parents for many years, and on Sundays would often ask to pop a small roast or joint into our oven to save his electric. This was not meant as tight or mean as much as merely a means to an end – from a man who had survived two world wars, and now lived alone... becoming what may be viewed as eccentric.

I adored him and I admired him for his logic. We once went to visit him in his new home, and as he made tea for us bunch of punks I noticed a pork pie... which he'd placed on a radiator to warm up for his tea! These people are the wonderful forgotten... and so often misunderstood by society.

Bless you, old Arthur.

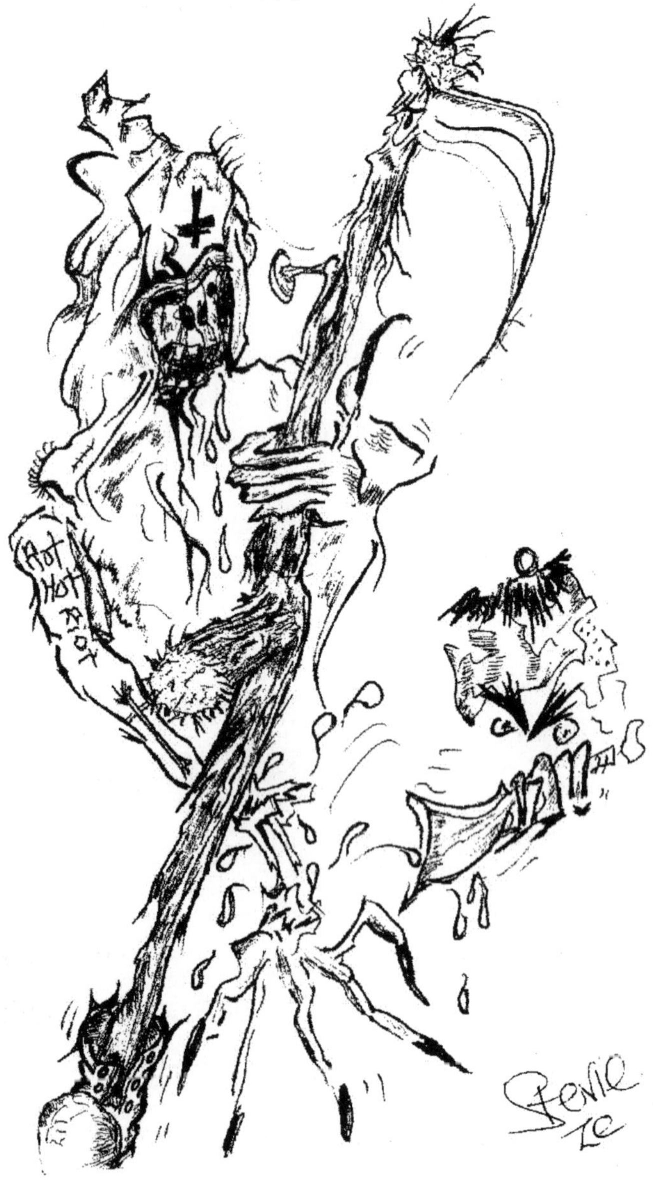
Hot
Hot
Riot

ROTTING CORPSE

The dead remain underground
They rot away without a sound
They stink as their flesh turns grey
And may move as their parts fall away
Fermentation of bone
With porcelain faces of stone
And the dead remain underground

Oblivious of what goes on
Lies a lifeless person now long gone
A sickening stench exudes from their head
Their eyes sink back 'til they're blackest death red
Decaying blue embers fill the torso
As the mouth explodes – a crimson floor show
The tongue expands 'til it protrudes with grace
Through the now blackened cheeks it once hid behind
Spewing out smelly dead blood
Through its now purple lips in true vampire style.

Blood red rivers of pain that trickle down now grey cheeks of a girl of seventeen. Once kissed to bits in love's sweet treat now lays asleep in slumbers deep.

I wonder how her auburn hair can look so lovely against her burial stare. I feel love for this girl who has lived and died before I even had a life. Wondered how she lived, how she cried, and why she died.

Never having seen a corpse so buried and forgotten for over one hundred years or so, I had a strange desire to ask – was she happy? Was she sad? Did she ever have any of the things we had?

> For her no Beatles, no Stones,
>
> No Dylan, no Ramones
>
> Did she love? Did she frown?
>
> Did she die without a sound?

I observed the lingering mindless glare of cadaver eyes like frozen ice cubes looking nowhere, as they must stare now at only a coffin lid entombed in total blackness.

> And within this now lifeless body of flesh
>
> There was once a person with mind so fresh
>
> Enjoying life for all it's worth
>
> Before lying here beneath the earth

And as time eats away 'til flesh becomes skeleton eroding life's most precious gift. She would have been so beautiful. Once so lovely. Once so feminine. I feel her heart divine, yet still beating, for her eternal solitude has now arrived.

I AM A MOTH

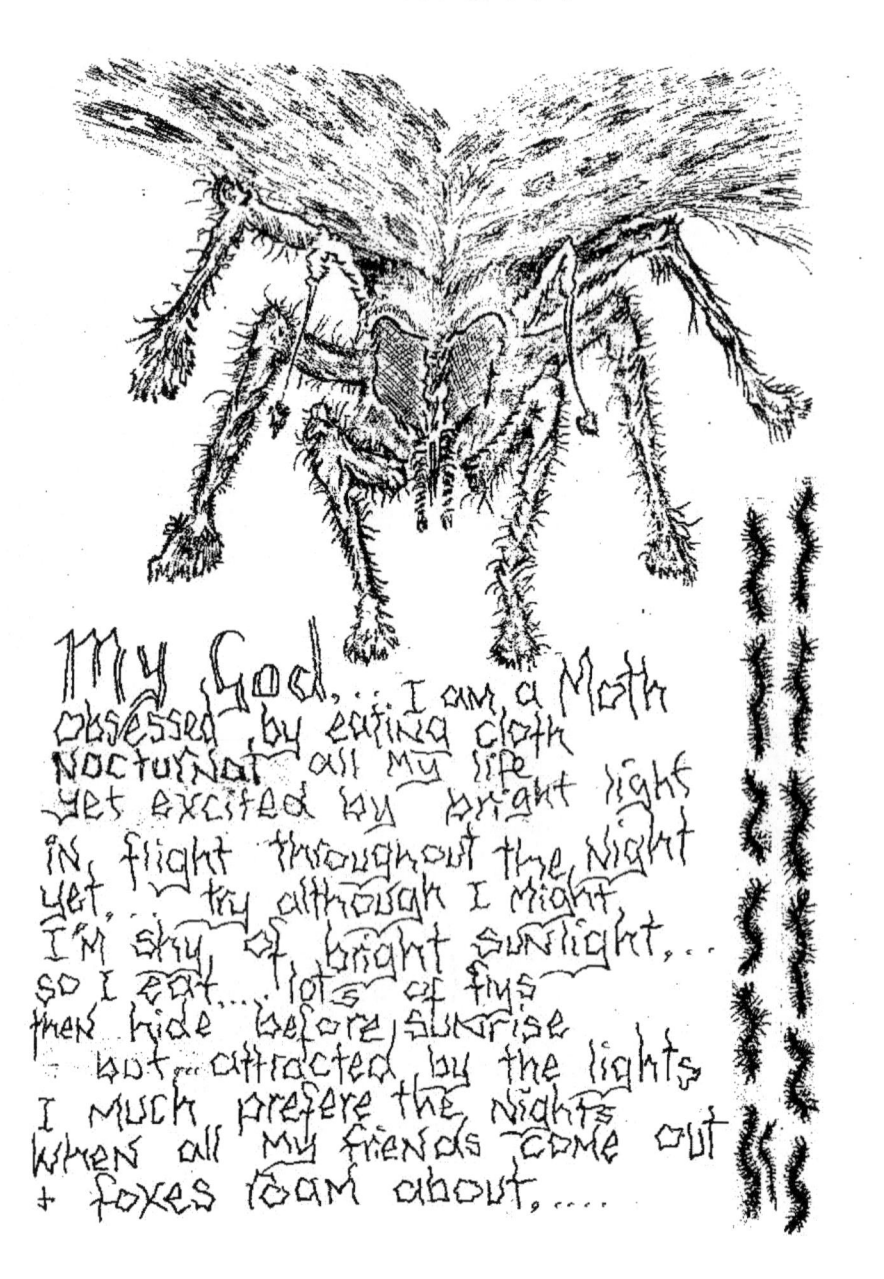

My God... I am a Moth
obsessed by eating cloth
Nocturnal all my life
yet excited by bright lights
in flight throughout the night
yet... try although I might
I'm shy of bright sunlight...
so I eat... lots of flys
then hide before sunrise
  but... attracted by the lights
I much prefere the nights
when all my friends come out
+ foxes roam about,....

Beneath a billion stars
as if theres life on Mars
& grubs are hot to trott
I'd like to eat the lot...
I'd like to eat some beans
but I'm not sure what bean meanz
so save me some more cloth
so I can munch away non-stop
yes I'm just a Moth
and to me.. life means a lot !!!

DESPAIRING

Despairing

I wish I could swim

I wish I could swim like you

I wish I could try - but I'll sink

To the bottom of the ocean

And disappear from view

Without even goodbye

Despairing

I wish I could fly

I wish I could fly like you

Fly through the sky

But I'd fall

Down to the ground

Straight through the clouds

Without even a sound

When you're sick from the promises

Left for dead by the lies

Disillusioned and confused

And so empty inside

Despairing

I wish I could run

I wish I could run like you

I wish I could try

But I'll trip

I'll stumble and fall

Straight to the floor

Just like before

    Despairing

    Oh how I wish I could swim

    I wish I could swim like you

    I wish I could try

    But I'm sunk

    And at the bottom of the ocean

    With this heavy load pressing down

    And such pressure all around.

I HAVE A DREAM

"I have a dream" – the wise words of Dr Martin Luther King – and how we have chosen to ignore them.

However – we can't ignore him!

As I witness this world of hateful xenophobic territoriality battles and mass misuse of power. Plus seemingly endless futile wars, usually over a God that probably does not even exist!

As I witness all these things I can't help but despair for the future of our beautiful planet, with all her wonderful animals, for the decent side of humanity, our children and our childrens' children. So now – as long as I have breath in my body – I will continue to fight against the sublime hypocrites and pimps, two-faced music thieves, and vile religious prejudice – the self-opinionated Christian church mice (the human kind, that is), small, one-upmanship snobs in their little villages, all the animal cruelty cowards – foxhunters, pheasant shooters, rabbit trappers, and money grabbers, internet trolls, social segregation bigots, gagging orders on our freedom of speech for which so many perished to maintain – and now the East takes it away, political correctness gone mad!

Thug-ruled mob mentality, brainless creeps, plus workplace and schoolyard cowardly bullies... oh, and tribute acts!

VILLAGE OF PEACE

The haunting willow weeps
The creeping reaper sneaks
As the quiet village sleeps
And dawn begins to creep

Whilst the dead lie
In eternal slumber
Beneath the silent graveyard
Seeped in wonder

Machine gun owls
May toot and tell
As mist descends
The wishing well

And on the village green

A fox is seen

What beauty surrounds

This elegant being

my darling foxy
foxy fox
across the village

Bottle tops and bumble bees

Benches made from ancient trees

Cockerel gives his morning song

Now all the birds will sing along

Steady milkman

Does his round

Completes his work

Without a sound

So still and tranquil

The village pond

Breeds life so rife

Where frogs belong

And deep below

Their tadpoles grow

Tiny legs and arms

Begin to show.

Parades of idyllic

Lilies shy

Hide baby ducks

In shades of rye

And on the glass-like

Water's edge

Marauding midges

Hatch their eggs

The local priest

Prepares her sermon

Amidst her flock

Of ragged mermen

As midday approaches
Bells will ring
Peals of hope
Show signs of spring

These bells of hope
Won't go unnoticed
But may be heard
As peaceful protest

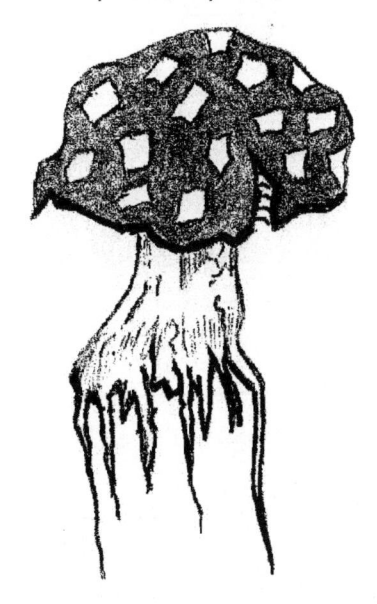

Beside the bus stop
Flowers grow
As daffodils
Of yellow glow.

Soon morning dew will sweep the land
And create fresh beauty no man could plan

Across these fields
Of peace now grow
In final frost
Of winter's glow

For in this land of England's green
With pleasant hillsides overseeing
Smiling down for all to see
Dripping shades of empathy

freddie frog
relaxes

Thus we are blessed by nature's ways
Which we must treasure all of our days.

Mysteries from the lake

BLACK SABBATH

I remember whilst recording an album down at Rockfield Studios in Monmouth, South Wales, I would regularly get up nice and early in order to be at the paper shop – and timing things just right so that I could cadge a lift from studio owner and first class chap, Kingsley Ward, in his gold Rolls Royce.

Now it's not like me to be impressed by flash cars – except when used in the context of rock 'n' roll posing! I have been known to be quite partial of the odd participation! Anyway, after years of travelling in the back of a shite old Transit van, with four or five other smelly, hairy blokes, all smokin' their heads off… the thought of a little luxury can be rather appealing – as well as a comfortable start to the day.

So I arrive feeling good for my paper and early morning beer buzz. All sheer pose, you understand – shades on, hair dyed, nail polish… the whole technique. But that's how I was – and probably still am!

Anyway, on this occasion I was accompanied by punk drummer Ice N, and we found ourselves in the company of none other than bass player Geezer Butler of Black Sabbath, who were also recording there. We were discussing this whilst standing behind him in the queue – a rock God!

We immediately struggled to see which paper he bought to read – shallow though this may seem, and I thought I was so deep, as well – oh well, that's just little old star-struck me, I suppose. Disappointingly for me was his choice of The Guardian, as I had originally picked up The Sun. "What no page three?"

So I never got one, but Geezer. 'Rock God', smiled at us as we climbed back into our borrowed Rolls with the wonderfully funny Kingsley, who found this whole episode very amusing.

What a morning's result!

Years later and it's UK Subs days now, Top of the Pops and chart positions had been conquered and I ended up with our tour manager Chutch and a couple of friends having a pint with Sabbath in the pub next door to one of their anniversary shows at the Hammersmith Odeon. Geezer was quite amused at my little story, and later gave us a smile and a nod from up on stage… though I think he had a quiet laugh about us really!

And I still like page three!! And Sabbath are among the nicest and best people I have met in my career!

COFFIN CHRONICLES

I see a coffin - it is a play
A play in which I die
And nothing help – "til life expires
However hard we try

I see a playground - full of fun
A playground soaked in pain
Of hopeless dreams - which fade away
Then perish in the rain

I see a birth - for what it's worth
Consumed in Hell we cry
'Til death ensues - our walking dead
Reach up to touch the sky

I see a grave - a grave too full
Ambitions brushed aside
Whatever tranquil peace dwells here
Awaits in Death's surprise

SONGBIRD OF LIFE

There's a songbird who sings
As if that song was meant for me
She calls me in the morning
Then again in time for tea

Amidst the traffic howling
And pollution you can see
She sings out loud her song of love
Whilst flying safe and free

I hope you never leave us
Or end up pushed away
We really need that song of love
To help us through each day

So carry on my darling bird
With wings to fly so high
I need to hear you every day
For without your song we'd die

our beautiful songbird 🖤

and chicks in their nests of future wildlife

BAY CITY ROLLERS

The first punks?

One of the highlights of my life was when I was asked to stand in on bass guitar for the Bay City Rollers.

This was a huge thrill and honour for me as, although a punk, I had always loved and admired their careers and those wonderful songs which they produced - one after the other and so many topped the charts!

In fact I saw them, as I know many others did, as the first punk band and ambassadors in the evolution of excellent entertainment. They defied all those cynics and jealous musicians and 'done-fuck-all' critics all rattling around in the cesspit of their own dung, absolute jack shite misery – while the girls all screamed for the Rollers! Fabulous poetry!

This, for me was going to be well good…

Well – I hadn't actually played bass guitar before at this point so I asked my producer, David Bowie's legendary Ziggy Stardust bass player Trevor Bolder, for a few tips!

Now I don't know if you all know this but my all-time favourite American band – the mighty Ramones – were huge Rollers fans and wrote their hit song Blitzkreig Bop, with the line 'Hey ho, Let's go' based on Bay City Rollers' S.A.T.U.R.D.A.Y.

I was in my element but quite down at this point, yet being back on stage, especially with the likes of Eric Faulkner, and thumping out all their hits with him, was just the tonic I needed at the time. A huge pick-me-up desperately essential to my self-esteem.

I met up with Eric in Hastings, down on the South coast, at Mike and Terri's Little London Studios in Candycane Alley. Everyone was so kind and helpful, and I immediately felt so at home there. I was asked to sign the wall of fame alongside Eric, and Poly Styrene (X Ray Spex), Jimmy Pursey (Sham 69), Mitch Mitchell (Jimi Hendrix Experience) and others.

Time for a cuppa at Little London Studios, Candycane Alley

When Eric greeted me he referred to me affectionately as 'Stevie Bod' – which was quite weird as this had been my nickname at school.

At our first show Roy wood and Wizzard were playing on the bill. Roy was equally as nice and friendly, giving me lots of support and confidence, so I had a picture taken with him.

It was a gig to remember and felt so good to once again be in the company of professionals on a big stage. We went on to play about an hour with songs which included 'Shang-a-lang', 'Summerlove Sensation', 'Give a Little Love', and so many more, plus, of course the incredibly brilliant, 'Bye Bye Baby' – each a hit record.

What an experience for me to add to an already event-filled Stevie Ze career!

SCOTT WALKER

I once had the privilege of meeting up with pop superstar Scott Walker of The Walker Brothers.

I found him to be a fascinating person of great artistic knowledge. We sat and chatted mainly about our mutual admiration and respect for French artist and songwriter, poet and performer Jacques Brell, who's song 'My Death' was covered by both Scott and David Bowie during Bowie's infamous live Ziggy Stardust shows, and has a lyric which has fascinated both of us for decades. Neither of us were sure where Brell was edging with it, yet he transported us to a new level of meaning – and Scott Walker, like David Bowie, has never been afraid of extreme expression in art.

I learned so much from just talking with him and realized I was in the company of a true super-talent who didn't fear the abyss of rejection, nor took any notice of the shallow companies or people who simply cannot see the bigger picture with all their ifs and buts. Both Scott Walker and David Bowie have taught me that there is a far greater depth to true artistic content than may meet the naked eye!

Scott Walker, you were so kind and generous with your experience and influence on me that day, which I have never forgotten and for which I thank you.

Never fear the unexplainable but use it

As a doorway of light.

Stevie Ze

I have been a lucky, lucky man to have lived through, and witnessed, so much wonderful music and performance. Like the amazing Louis Armstrong, Jimi Hendrix, Mama Cass, and on through, Scott Walker, Jacques Brell, Edith Piaf, Sid Vicious and David Bowie. A very varied mixture – but none of whom carried one ounce of fear – yet touched me so deeply.

I have been a lucky, lucky man!

NEIL SEDAKA

One of the most inspiring artists I ever met was the lovely Neil Sedaka, who was so endearingly polite and, above all, extremely encouraging to me.

When my Dad, a pianist and Musical Arranger, worked with him at Batley Variety Club during the seventies he took me with him. He would often take me along just for the company as he grew older, and on this occasion, for these shows, he was playing piano – Sedaka's grand piano out on centre stage.

He would run on and take over the piano every time Neil Sedaka stood up to the front of stage mic stand to sing. I worked a treat and I was very proud to see it!

The legendary Mr Sedaka spoke to me at length about song-writing and never allowing yourself to be put off by anyone. I have carried this through whilst doing exactly what I feel I have to do in music, without negative interruption. He had all the time for helping me, busy though he was. "And never forget the odd drop dead chord," he told me. "What's that?" I asked, and he taught me all about it. "In a verse, chorus, or middle eight, there will be a chord – maybe not a correct natural progression, yet somehow just manages to fit in – and can touch people's inner emotions. It's a fascinating concept which actually works a treat and I have used to great advantage on several occasions – such as my track with Trevor Bolder, 'Wild Trash', using A to F – a similar chord sequence formerly used in the Bond theme for 'Goldfinger'.

Neil Sedaka – a truly genuine songwriter and performer who is so passionate about his craft.

Shortly after this I bought Carole King's 'Tapestry' album, a fabulously inspiring work of sheer art.

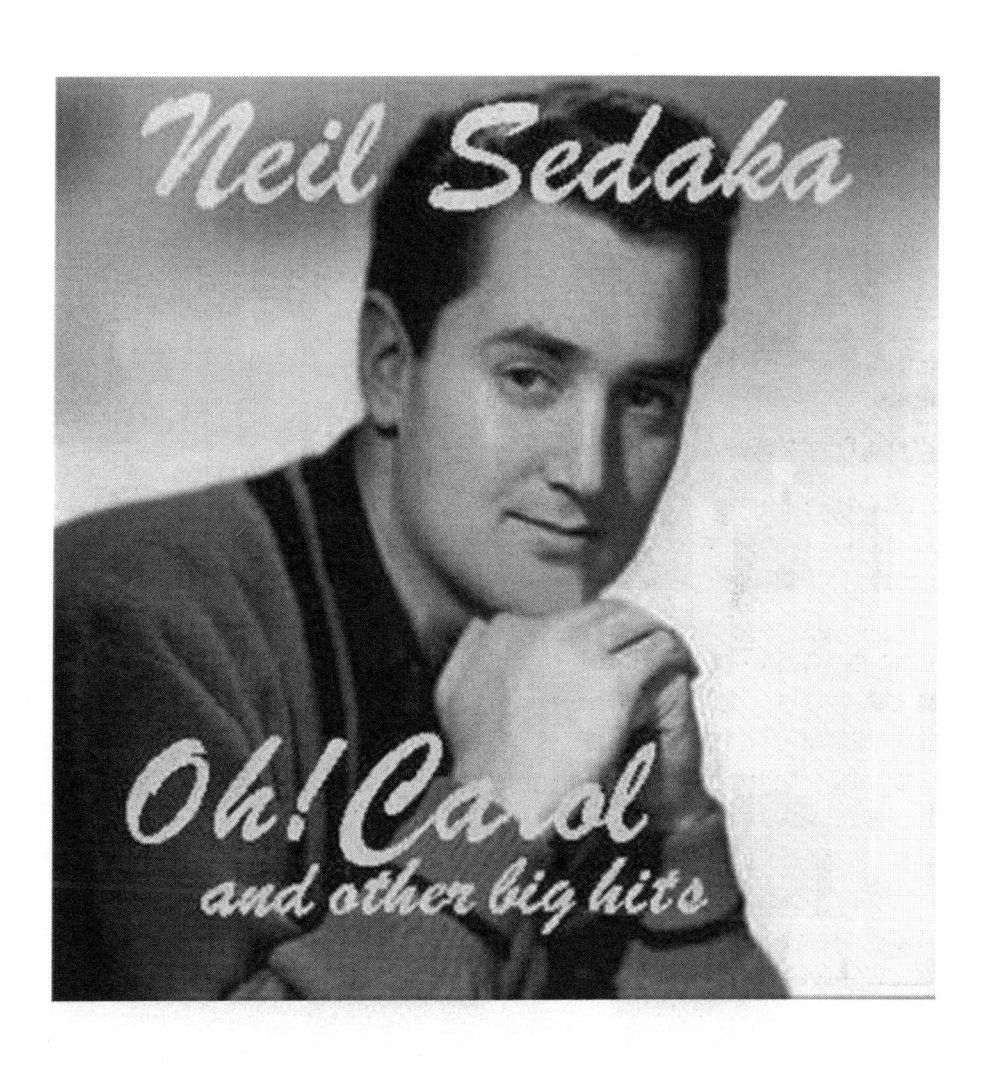

PERSONALITY DISORDER, ANXIETY, DEPRESSION AND ALCOHOL

A will to survive

A way to survive

Personality disorder causes isolation and solitude and an inability to comfortably coexist with the rest of society.

Anxiety can result in frightening panic attacks and constant worry over just about anything at all, often with a violent sick feeling of nausea mixed with fear.

Depression is a crippling illness that can effect anyone at any time – without warning!

So, by now, dependence on alcohol had become a very useful crutch to lean on. However, BEWARE, alcohol can be a useful brick wall to hide behind – as it was with me – but it can so easily creep up on you and take over just like the black cloud of sheer peril that it is.

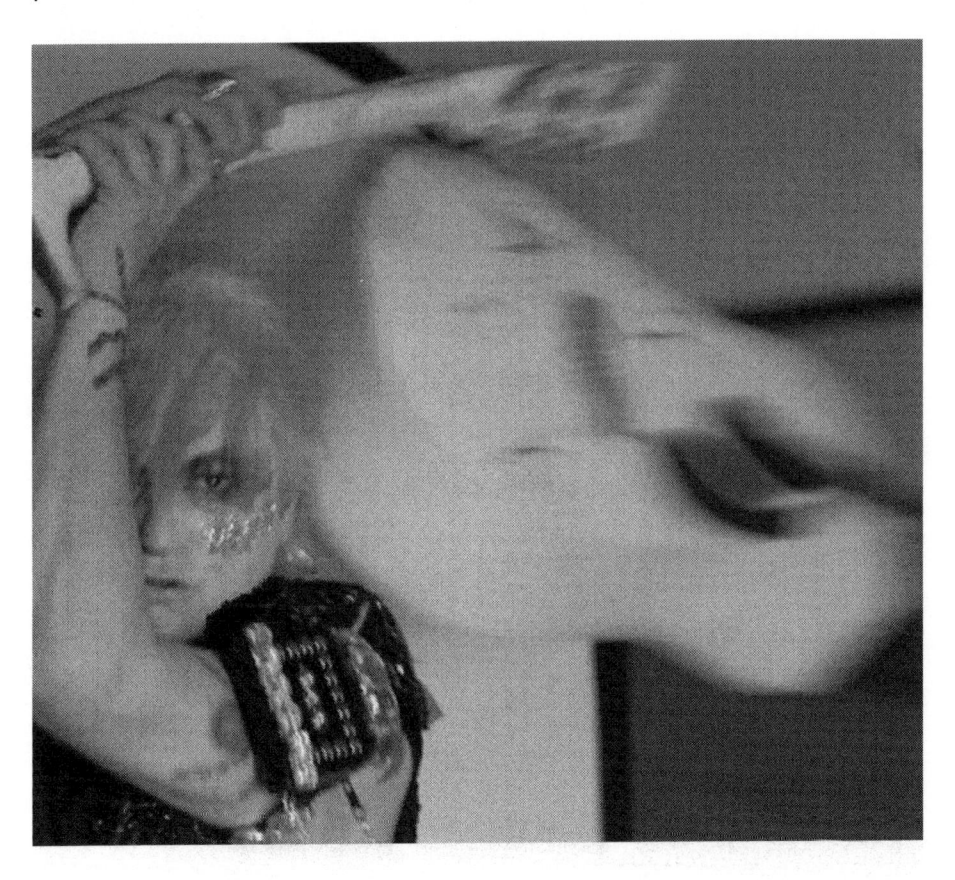

My guitar is like an audible weapon

Dark clouds may follow you

Rain falls on all you do

Fate drapes its darkest cape

Across your heart of gold.

                                                Stevie Ze

And all this misery and suffering is bought on usually through stress caused by numerous human situations…

Bullying, rudeness, ignorance, constant uncalled for criticism, name calling, racism, homophobia, and basic all-round prejudice from pre-judgemental energy vampires, and those usually as narcissistic as they are shallow!

Well, these patronizing persons must no longer be allowed to infiltrate your mind or life… I mean – HOW DARE THEY? And who the Hell are they anyway? With their narrow minded blind bigotry and vicious innuendos. Not to mention that frustratingly cruel and selfish passive aggression that they just love to practice… shunning or shutting out and ignoring a certain individual until they inevitably crack!

This silent treatment screams out so loud at you – a silent hurricane of mental torture until you'll inevitably burst with sheer frustration… and then, of course, it's all YOUR fault! And don't they just love it when you break!

Often this is the moral majority's only power over those they resent – the most vulnerable and sensitive, or the most talented, gifted or clever.

They hurt you at home – they hit you at school

They hate you if you're clever – they despise a fool

'Til you're so fuckin' crazy – you can't follow their rules

John Lennon

Peace isn't in their vocabulary as they revel in petty vendettas and jealousy – so stay among nice gentle and intelligent people, who care about animals and are decent and respectful towards you! Let the haters rot in the Hell they create around themselves!

Remember –

"Not everyone likes you – but not everyone matters."

> Wild trash
> 22nd Century Noize
> Maximum Hype
> Exploitation
>
> Wild Noize
> sick loud Rock n' Roll,
> chaos, Anarchy
> + destruction,...
> the destruction of boredom!
>
> Noize Suicide

ARIZE FROM THE ABYSS

I had hit rock bottom after a wonderful career which I adored – to eventually realize what all this hatred and resentment around me was doing to me.

My manager, Mike Harris, said to me, "Sit down and write a book – put everyone in it who's hurt you. Get it all off your shoulders." So I did – this is the book – I let it all out, and so can you.

Don't let the haters win – the cynics, the critics – who are they anyway? Ask yourself, more importantly, what are they? What great yahoo deed have they ever achieved in order to qualify to put *you* down?

I'll answer that for you – most probably NOTHING! And that's why you are such a threat to them and therefore a target for their abuse.

Writing this took such a huge weight off my shoulders I once again felt free to continue my artistic quests without persecution or puts downs from people who delight in causing pain. Yet it was like living in a nightmare at first – doors slammed in my face, local musicians using me for contacts in the industry, two-faced back stabbers and users all around! But you just need to learn to override them all. Hardship is the price of an education, you can learn from all the blows and, most importantly, you learn how to spot the instant bozo or two like I did!

Musicians and business cretins picking fault in everything they hear for the sake of looking clever – which is most probably why they remain small fry, tiny fishes in an even smaller micro-pond.

But you can more than often use the hurt they inflict on you as a weapon against them by gaining strength from the pain, be it later in life or whenever. Remember they'd love to see you lose so don't give them that satisfaction – this is a fabulous incentive to get back onto your feet after a fall. I know it was for me!

There is nothing more sickening than the absolute 'know-it-all' control freak who'll lead anyone down the garden path solely for their own benefit.

You know I was told once by one local bozo that I could never write a song or play a guitar like he can. A total clever dick who no longer exists in any part in my life any more – just one of many who tried to stop and destroy me... but failed.

By building an imaginary brick wall around you to keep the blank negative ones out you will be much more able to keep your artistry and passions alive – be it music, animals, fashion, sport, care of others, poetry, children's well-being, or whatever you want, without any pre-installed doubt placed in your mind by anyone.

One particular nuisance predator has followed me throughout my career in order to rip me off and try to ruin me – that same conman is instinctively engraved in my mind, and always will be, but he won't beat me!

"I'm just an individual who doesn't feel the need to have anybody qualify my work in any particular way. I'm working for me."

David Bowie

"Be happy and content with your life." Stevie Ze

"Be at one with yourself." Bruce Lee

YOU ARE NOT ALONE

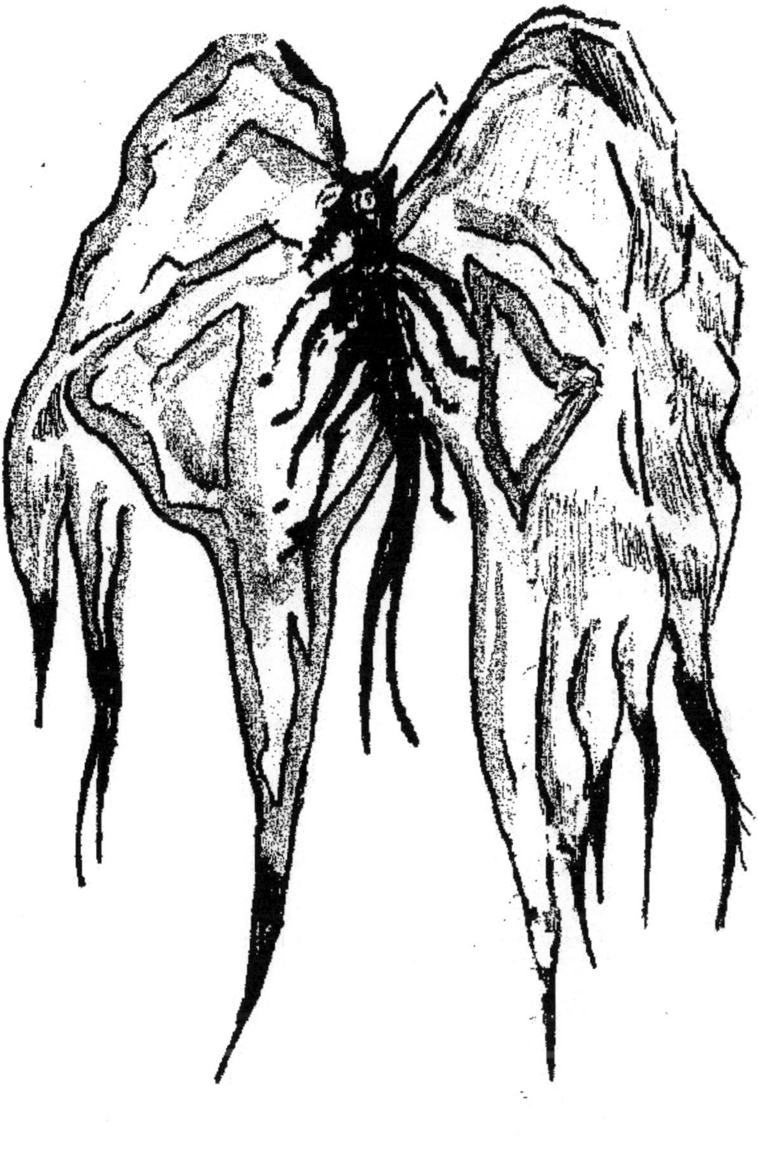

UK SUBS (PART 1)

Working in a band like UK Subs was a revelation of just how a real band should be. I'm talking about the lineup consisting of Charlie Harper (of course), Nick Garrett on guitar, Alvin Gibbs on bass, and myself, Stevie Ze on drums.

The action-packed shows were unreal, and for me a beautiful dream come true for each member was a star in their own right and that is how I learned so much. When I joined we desperately needed a bass player. No-one seemed suitable then in walked Alvin Gibbs, complete with eye-liner and, best of all, low-slung – extremely low-slung – bass guitar. He had a picture of Marc Bolan on his amp, and I though "Fabulous", this boy is a star.

Immediately we started to play there was a very special energy, especially from Nick Garrett whose stage presence and performance were electrifying all the time. The lineup was then complete and we started out on a sixty-three date British tour.

The current album hit the charts and we were soon doing Top of the Pops. The first gig was Cardiff Top Rank, a huge venue with a large balcony – and there were almost as many people outside, unable to get in, as there was inside!

The dressing rooms were underneath the stage and to hear three thousand or so young feet stamping and shouting "UK Subs. UK Subs" was quite deafening – if not a little scary!

Manager Mike Philips said to me, "Okay, son, you're the new boy – up you go. Good luck." And so I was first on stage. As I climbed those steps and sat in on my drum kit amidst this wonderful, deafening chanting I felt very emotional and excited. Adrenaline was on room service now as the crowd went absolutely wild when I appeared. I started playing as the others walked on then we launched straight into C.I.D. and the whole of this fabulous venue erupted into pure energy – what a tremendous feeling!

After the show we were driven off to our posh hotel, half deaf, with ears ringing, favourite cocktail in hand, towel around the neck and a wonderful feeling inside. Back at the hotel more fans were waiting and we sat and talked with them for hours about our favourite bands. It was lovely!

Charlie Harper was, and still is, such a brilliant front man and songwriter. I learned so much from him. In fact, the whole band had a special quality and I miss them all on a daily basis. I'm very proud to have been a part of a band with these guys – the best days of my life!

FRAGILE BUTTERFLY

Young caterpillars crawling by
Who someday soon will reach the sky
On powdered wings of wonderment
In silent flight of pure contentment.

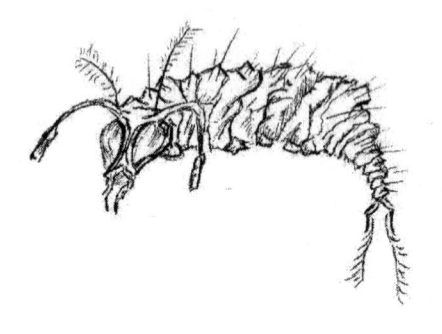

Red Admirals may also be
That lost relation back to see
A distant loved one from the past

Taken from us, is home at last.

From chrysalis to open skies

On gentle wings of steel she flies

Such delicate and silent strength

To lift us all in sweet lament.

Adorned with pastel colours bright

This purely visual delight

What tranquil moments she so inspires

For all your presence I never tire.

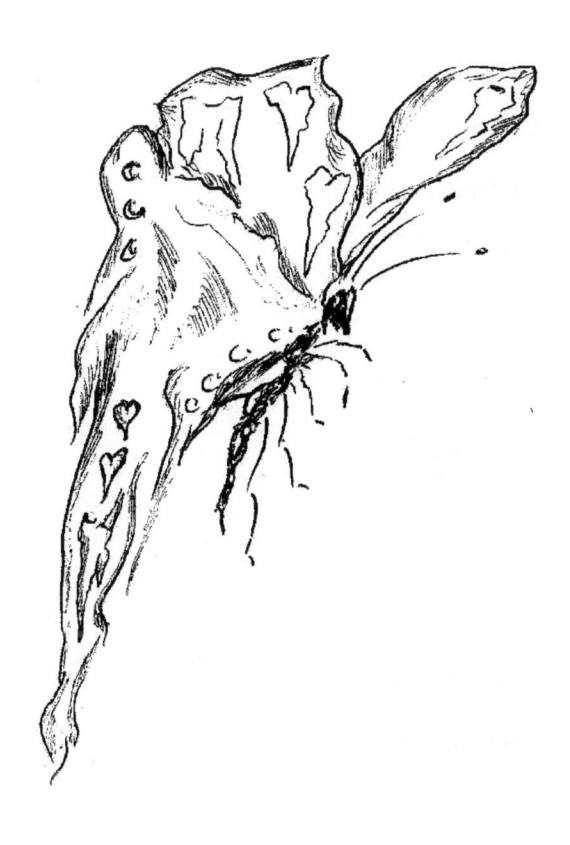

My heart is broken, my demons many
Yet how you stir my heart so heavy
My friendships cold, my body old
Rough talent sold, or so I'm told

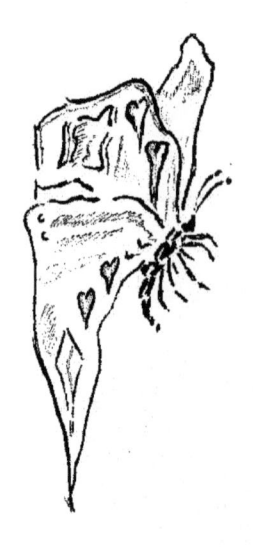

Yet our archetypal butterfly
Will flutter by and fly so high
On velvet wings across the oceans
Worlds away from life's commotions

Like flowing poetry gliding by
We can't deny you, butterfly
So free and silent in the sky
You truly are sweet… butterfly

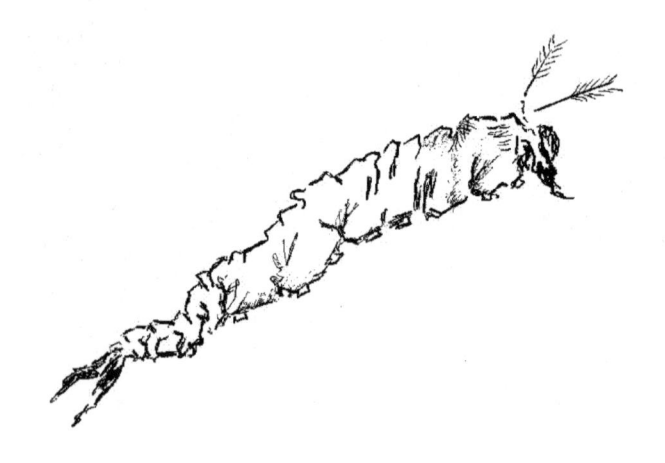

THE DEAD

the dead
sink their claws in me
the living
steal the air I breath
and leppers
pick their days
in careful pain

the smell of death
around a suicide
do pretty flowers
make you wanna cry
as satan spreads his wings
and calls your name.

DRAGONFLY

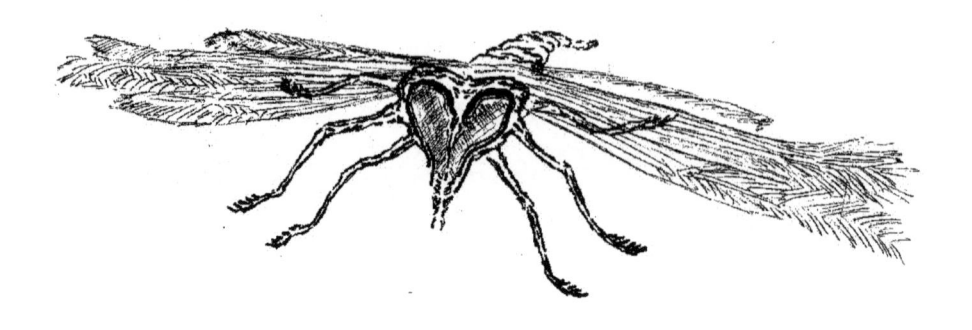

Dragonfly you only get

A day or two to live

Yet in that time you grace

The finest pleasure life can give

You're a helicopter humming bird

Of decadent desire

A ballerina of the air

Intense and full of fire

You only have
Such little time
To flaunt your fine display
And there you are for just a moment
Then you're gone away

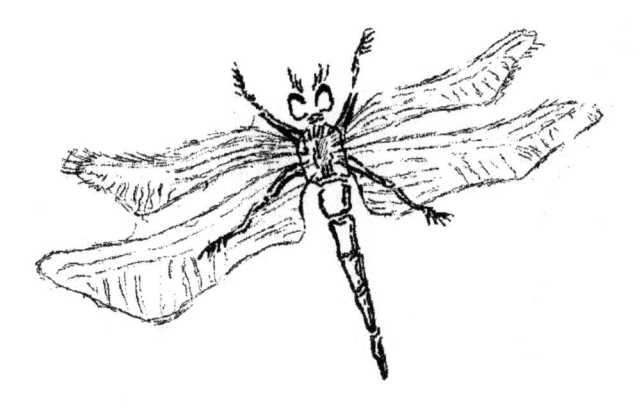

With silent wings of wonderment
And flying skills immense
How can we all ignore
Such acrobatic excellence?

I wait to greet you next year
In the children you'll create
Who'll skim the ground with stealth-like ease
Young warriors at lightning speed

Dragonfly, you're still the greatest

Aviator of the ages

So glorious, with flag unfurled

The finest airman in the world.

"Per adru ad astra"

Royal Air Force motto

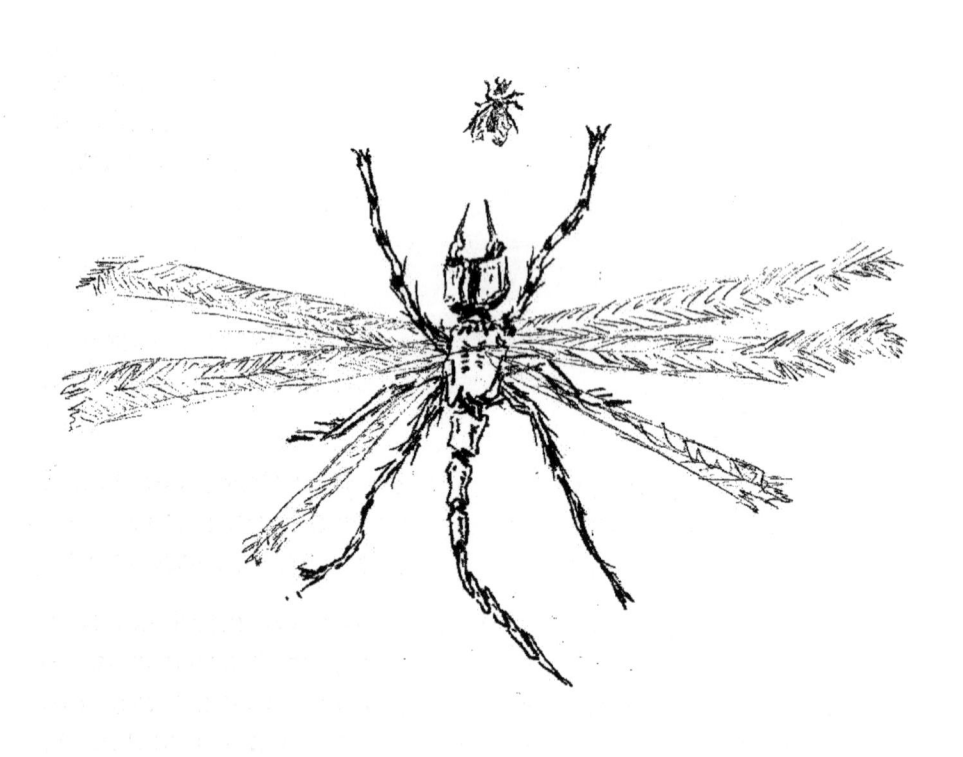

BRUCE LEE'S DEFENCE TECHNIQUE

You know, a simple smile is a mighty powerful weapon for turning the tables on your aggressor or aggressors, thus allowing their negativity, hatred or piss taking attempts to just skim off you and merely make you smile even more!

We all possess an invisible built-in protection system – rather like the Earth's atmospheric layer preventing entry of anything which could be potentially dangerous to our planet. However, we rarely use this human force field – mainly as we are not necessarily aware that it exists!

Yet, believe me it does – and a simple smile with an otherwise zero reaction, you will find, is just the trick for disarming a bully.

As the brilliant martial artist and philosopher Bruce Lee would teach "Soft is hard." It took me ages to work out just what he meant by this, yet once I'd got it, I could see how correct he was.

You see, to react back angrily to either verbal or physical abuse you are only creating a stalemate situation, which can only go on to result in a bigger verbal or physical confrontation. A negative equity of fruitless combat. Plus, of course, lowering yourself to their level. Whereas, to calmly react with "Oh sorry. I'm sorry you feel that way, as I think you're a really good person," or something to that effect disarms the aggressor and, at the same time, makes them appear rather foolish and sad.

This technique works a treat. Bruce Lee was an extremely gifted and wise man to get it so spot on – "Soft is hard."

And as for the vile ignorant persons who may shout loudly straight at you, or in your face, just remember that shouting is only volume. I know it can be quite frightening, like when an extremely loud aircraft flies overhead…But it is only VOLUME!

Empty vessels make the most noise. (Anon)

Words, even if shouted, are only empty hot air, usually from a person who lacks the intelligence to discuss or argue in a civilized manner.

This can be disarmed so easily by a gentle, quiet response before simply walking away and leaving the hot-head with nothing except a failed attempt to cause upset.

SOFT IS HARD (*Bruce Lee*) – learn it!

My Beloved doggies are everywhere and fill my life with Love

JIMMY PURSEY

"Robin 'Ood, Robin 'Ood, 'Ere we are again!"

When this great frontman and performer, Jimmy Pursey, hit the Top of the Pops stage this was his cheeky opening line – and with his fabulously exciting band Sham 69 they reached Top of the Pops again and again. Despite jealous back-stabbing critics they presented sheer entertainment performing their own songs written by Jimmy and guitarist Dave Parsons.

Great hits like 'If the Kids are United.' (used by Tony Blair at a Labour conference), 'Hersham Boys,' 'Hurry Up Harry,' (rewritten into Hurry Up England for the 2006 World Cup), 'Borstal Breakout, (used in the film 'Rise of the Footsoldiers) and many more.

Well, that's what I call a class act! Jimmy Pursey – your music legacy will live for ever.

Jimmy Pursey at Victoria Park 2008 Rock against Racism festival

VIETNAM

In the back streets of Naples
I was taught to be stable
Amongst the GI's of Vietnam
To the rat burgers of Uncle Sam.

From the poufs and queers and engineers
To their sweaty sexual homophobic fears
The hookers, the lookers,
The dealers, the stealers.

I ate my pizza every morning
Awaiting the aircraft carriers arriving
To blast the Vietnamese to death
Then frequent the club to fight the rest.

Welcome to the dark world of THE TIGER CLUB.

I'd been sent with a band to play in Naples. The Vietnam War was raging and Naples was a R & R stop-off for American GI's.

What followed was a hard education in survival.

During the Vietnam War US aircraft carriers would stop off and refuel in Naples harbour. The crew, who often hadn't seen land for months, would arrive ashore for some well-earned relaxation. Enter "Lady Barbie of Naples." And what a welcome they received – girls, food, wine, beer... and Barbie!

We named her Lady Barbie of Naples lady as she would sit by the dock and provide her oral services as the ships came in. Dispensing waste into her leopard skin covered bucket she would announce "Next!" as the sailors stood in line smiling, with their Yankee dollars ready in their hands.

Finally, the freshly unloaded matelots would proceed to the infamous 'Tiger Club' for a beer and a good old fashioned fight – and fantastic fun was had all round. Inside the club chairs would fly as bloody battles broke out on just about an hourly basis.

There was no chicken wire mesh to protect the band on stage but then the band wasn't the target – which seemed to be just each other! Aside from all this they were all regular friendly Americans to us, in fact we never felt threatened or in danger.

It was here we met Lollipop Pete, a huge figure of a man, hard as nails, but always sucking a lollipop. He would fight three or four at a time, and when he'd beaten the shit out of them would quietly sit down with a beer and another lollipop and listen to our music.

This was truly a bizarre place to be but I loved it there. It was always full of beautifully strange characters, all on their way to war! Another senseless political war!

I would play and observe the next violent brawl erupt but would simply carry on playing as though nothing was happening. In the mornings I would cross the road from the club to the café for a coffee and a home-made pizza – made by my friends there, and that was the most wonderful pizza ever!

Every morning for six months I did this – every morning a pizza, every night a ratburger. The tough guys were everywhere but left us alone, in fact they were extremely protective of the makeup-wearing rock band in their midst! I felt safer there than anywhere, and was made very welcome by the Italian people – bless them all for being so lovely!

So – back to our GI's and another aircraft carrier arriving. Lady Barbie would be busy once more with her bucket on the dock.

The band would play. The boys would fight. In fact, the only time there would be complete silence was when the strippers came on. Then it was ultimate stillness and silence. You could have heard a pin drop as the girls walked off stage – but just for those two seconds, mind! Then another chair would fly across to the other side of the room and battle would commence once again.

I do believe they truly enjoyed themselves – occasionally stopping for a few beers before starting up again. Yet we must remember that these guys didn't know if they would ever see home again. I suppose a good fight got the worry out of their systems – I'll never know! There was such a strangely bizarre sadness about it all – a feeling of sadness I'll never forget.

"Bloody wars are no good!"

There was somewhat of a macabre surrealism surrounding this whole place – a living ghostly atmosphere, as if everyone was already dead. Just walking corpses, victims of war trapped in time and waiting to meet their death – in a kind of parallel universe to the rest of us who were at peace, and alive.

Yet these panicked kids were in the middle of some kind of nightmare warzone scenario, on their way to a likely death, or maybe even worse, all in the name of politics and beyond their control.

Young and old on both sides bound to die, and for what? A plot of land? Or merely leaders feuding over oil rights or money issues, I'll never understand for sure, but it all felt ugly as the political perpetrators sit down to a splendid expensive dinner at home, never seeing the madness or the anxiety of the soldiers going to the front line, following orders.

Well – I saw it, and it wasn't a pretty sight!

I wondered who would survive, these boys and girls of a love generation forced, some dragged, into conflict. My darlings, you all tried so hard to live yet were met only by disregard of your wishes. I've just described a strange living Hell on Earth. An apocalyptic playground of tension and stress – of people, mostly young people, possibly in their last weeks of life on Earth, thinking about loved ones back home. Facing the rockets and heavy shelling which inevitably devastates all sides – except, of course, the cowardly leaders who stay at home. Be it the aggressors or the innocent, the killers or the killed, the assassins or the assassinated…

"*Generals gather in their masses*

Just like witches at Black Masses."

Black Sabbath

And so we carry on. Never learning by our mistakes. Never thinking of others in hurt and pain and mental torture. I watched this Russian roulette commence.

I played endlessly in that club and I only hope we were a tonic to those possible future victims of war. At the same time I cry for the Vietnamese who actually hadn't done anything wrong at all, and as the innocent perished over there we played on – as expected. Then afterwards we'd pile down to the docks, as usual, for what can only be described as a probable ratburger, and as our GI's left for war, another lot would arrive, and Lady Barbie would reappear.

Life and death carry on – and it seems it always will.

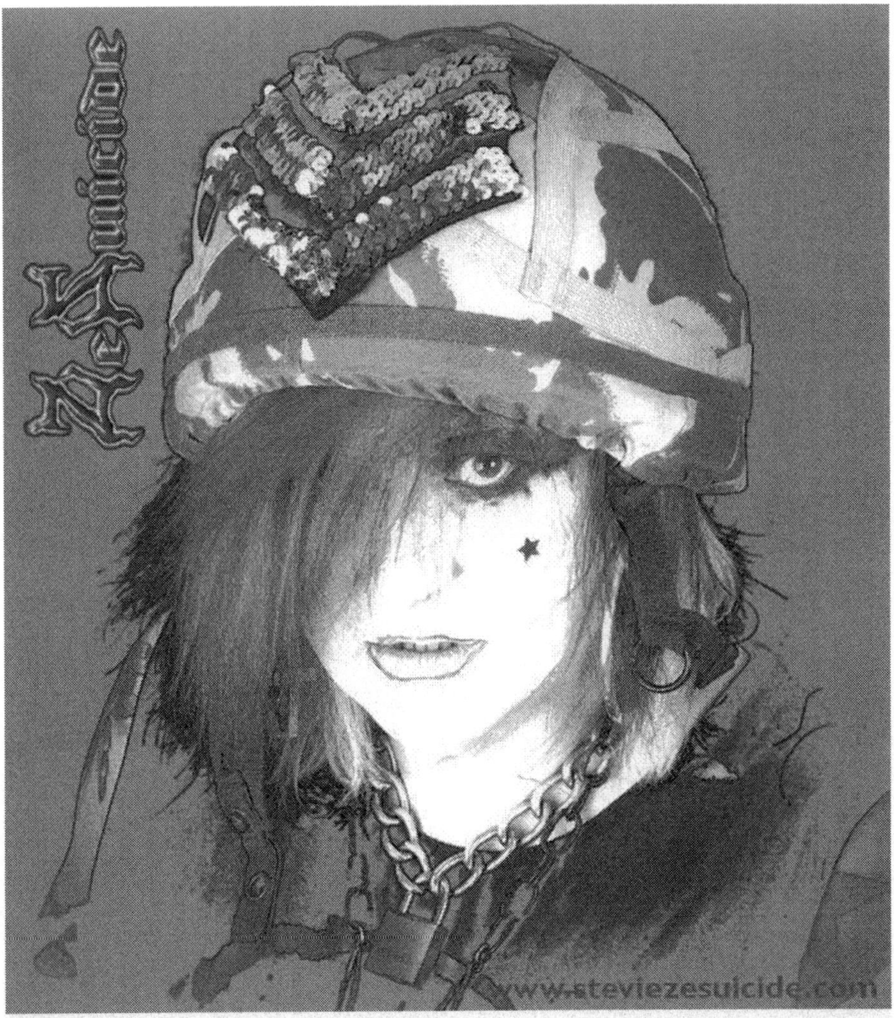
www.steviezesuicide.com

AWARDS OF EXCELLENCE

MP's are to be awarded with a prestigious new 'kill the poor' award for their services to elitism and general snotty public school lack of caring.

The award will be presented by the late Eva Braun through a medium. Catering will be supplied by TV chefs who will be serving up their favourite delicacies. Dolphin and 'live' foal served on a bed of powdered rhino horn, with a side of minced baby in an elephant tusk. Meals cost twenty five thousand pounds each, but are being paid for by the disabled, through benefit reductions and old age pensioners, through changes in the new BBC television licensing laws.

One female Labour MP will give a lecture on blonde-haired, blue-eyed chicks from Finland being employed as nurses in the NHS, rather than anyone from the Caribbean. It appears it's perfectly alright for her to preach this and not to be considered racist. One rule for one and another for everyone else!

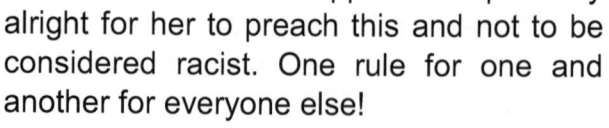

And the Golden Snot Award goes to…..

Bay City Rollers' singer Les McKeown for his unstarting respect and admiration of me and my music, His gentlemanly conduct surpasses imagination, as does his politeness. No-one deserves this prestigious award more than Les – who has now become a lifetime holder in perpetuity.

PSYCHO VICAR

I hope you can see from this book that you should not feel alone, that you are not the only person to be bought down by the powers that be, and that you can once again feel welcome, confident and happy in a world that doesn't seem to care. Religious encounters can be extremely hurtful and injurious to your health -- this is my true story.

Whilst I was writing my first book – Rock & Roll Chronicles – I would often seek solitude and inspiration wherever possible and, although not necessarily a religious person, I loved to find a quiet church in order to sit silently and soak up some peaceful atmosphere. One church in particular which I visited had a young man who practiced on the beautiful sounding church organ with its wonderful pipes and bellows. I was in blissful Heaven.

Then my Heaven was shattered and turned into sheer Hell, killing all my faith and respect, in the form of a lady vicar – an extremely harsh and aggressively bitter vicar. One day she found me sitting there and banged me on the shoulder shouting, "Out! Out! You can't sit in here! Out!" Then, because I took offence at this unwarranted outburst and told her so, I later found myself in court after she complained I had assaulted her. Where's the justice in that?

I was once asked to play in a church one Sunday. I arrived, met the band and plugged in. My choice of song was John Lennon's 'Imagine' – a song of peace if anyone takes the trouble to read the lyrics. However, as I began playing the opening verse, *'Imagine there's no Heaven'* a bigoted clever dick church mouse leaned patronizingly over me and said, "Inappropriate!" At this point I packed up and left.

This prejudgemental attitude that surrounds so-called Christians had kicked in once again. He was so full of enjoyment at causing hassle, with a clever smirk on his Jesus-filled face. It clearly pleased him so much!

So damn the self-opinionated, always so correct and perfect, blinkered and intolerant, rude and ignorant, beyond belief, terminally homophobic Christian bigots – twisting the Bible to whatever they want to read into it.

Years later, a very lovely lady invited me into her church for a very special service for alternative young people – I politely declined.

"I never really hated any one true God

But the God of the People I hated."

Marilyn Manson

"Bring me a choir boy!"

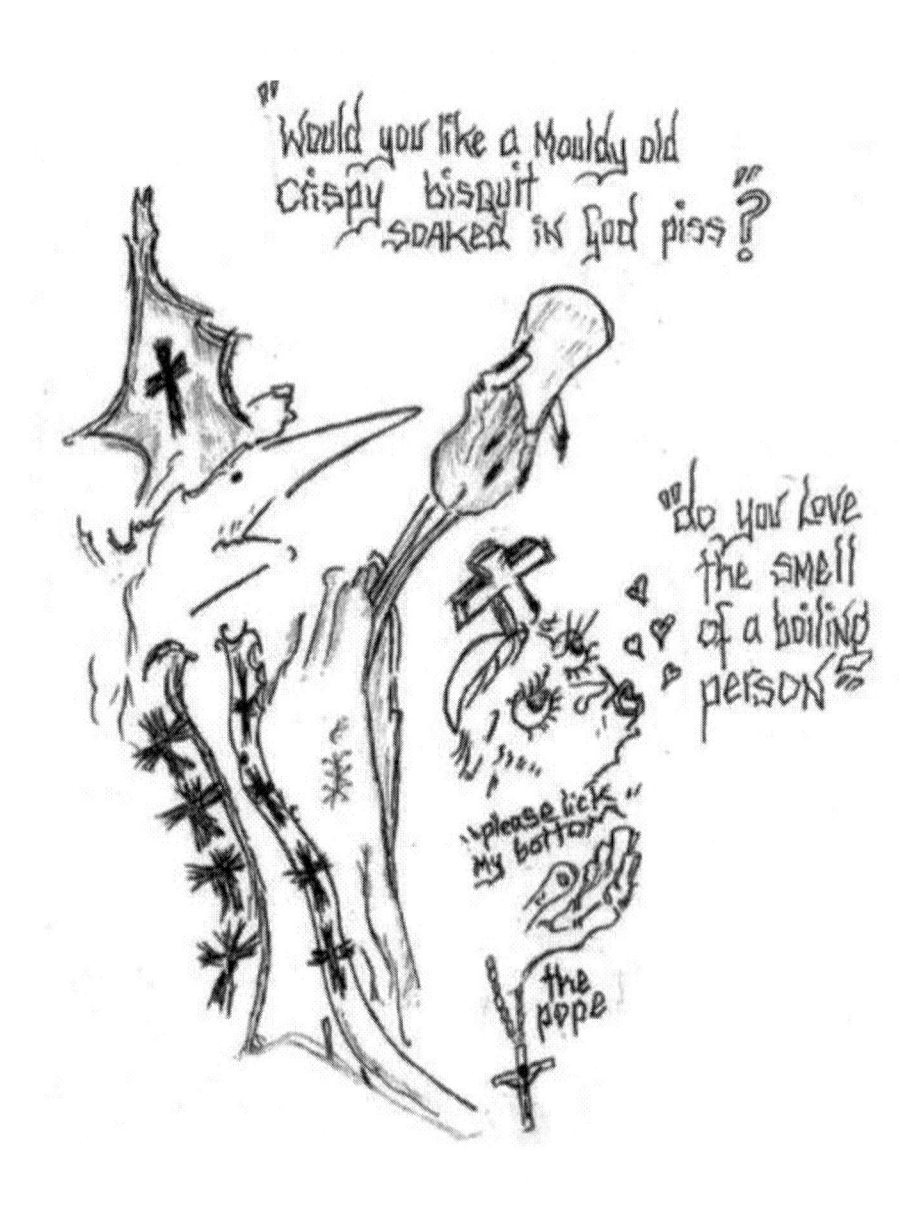

"Would you like a mouldy old crispy bisquit soaked in God piss?"

"Do you love the smell of a boiling person"

"please lick my bottom"

the pope

DEAD END STREET

One-way streets – boundary lines
Student fees and parking fines
Don't drive too fast – Keep off the grass
Don't eat this and don't say that.

Supermarket genocide – wheeler dealers
Corporate liars – egocentric paranoids
Hypocrites and verbal noise

Religious views – tabloid news
Buy this, pay that - you can't refuse
Exasperating bigotry
Sycophant celebrity.

Jobsworth red tape, narrow minds
Prejudgemental parasites
Don't stand here – you can't come in
Your hair's too long and you're way too thin

Gross moronic effigies

Billion dollar fantasies

Priests who hide their hidden crimes

Marauding lordies socialise

See Daddy's little chauvinist

With his golf club sickening materialists

All little people made of wood

But you can't go in if you look too good.

CLASSICAL PUNK

At a studio in Fulham or Chelsea I ran into Julian Lloyd Webber, cellist and classical maestro. We had a beer together and got on so well! We talked about the world of classical and punk music, and how some of the great composers were actually very much rebels of their time. I couldn't help but admire this man, not only for his immense genius but also his vast knowledge and understanding of art in its purest forms.

Another extremely interesting person, although I never actually met him, is composer Tim Rice with his superbly extensive knowledge of rock and roll. I didn't have him down as a rock and roller, but having listened to his radio broadcasts he certainly is – from Elvis Presley to Carl Perkins and Little Richard, etc.

I think it's wonderful how people from all different musical types and styles can come together without barriers, as one, to discuss alternative forms of expression through music and dance. And music and dance are vital, in my estimation, for breaking down social barriers.

We have fashion and dance, music and poetry, sculptures and art, magnificent actors and actresses, the ballet and the theatre.

> "A dreadlock bleach-blonde ice-cream smile
>
> In lizard leather plastic boots
>
> Nothing's ever what it seems
>
> But excuse me while I bleach my roots." Stevie Ze

DEATH OF A POET

A murdered swan

*"Be strong, be proud – you are beautiful
Each of you is a rainbow"*

Stevie Ze

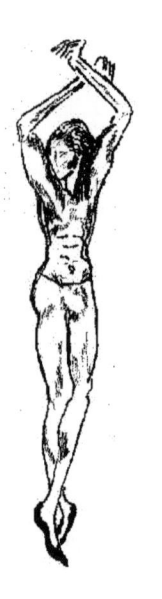

*To be nobody
To be someone
The death of a poet
A murdered swan*

*Amidst this age
Of talent show gloom
The end of art
By the panels of doom.*

*The crucifixion
By powers that be
Of originals, talent
And creativity.*

No music allowed
Just karaoke chancers
They even crush
Our wonderful dancers

To be nobody
To be someone
The death of a poet
A murdered swan

Though we try in vain
To wake up the dead
To all the books
They've never read

To all the words
They've never said
It seems so pointless
For they're all dead

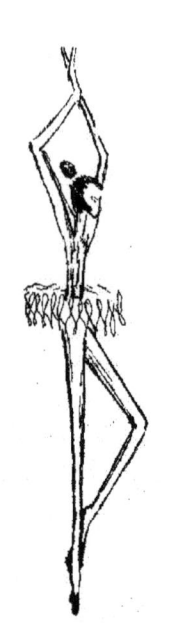

So tell me why
We don't belong
And tell me why
You think I'm wrong

And tell me why
You hate my song
As you watch me die
Like the murdered swan.

"the death of a poet is a murdered swan"

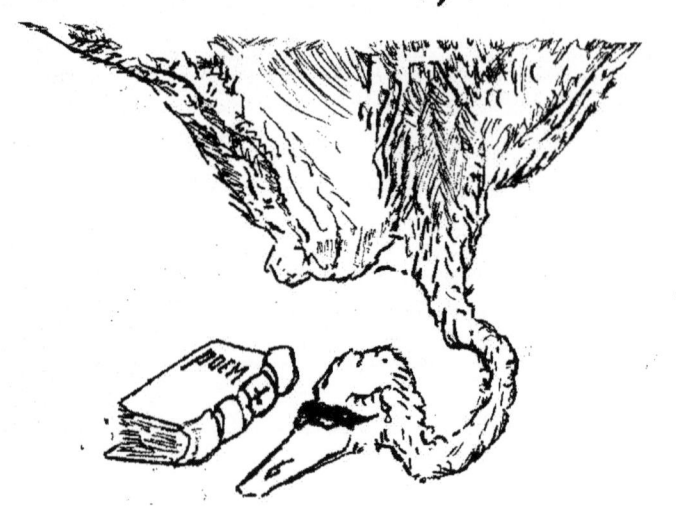

BRIAN MAY

The nicest, most respectful and lovely person I have been lucky enough to meet and spend time with is Queen's brilliant guitarist Brian May.

Not only a genius on guitar but also a well-qualified astrophysicist, and a lifelong lover of nature and all animals. He has been a patron of societies protecting both foxes and badgers,

He is superbly caring and gentle. A real example of how people should be in this world of ours – as indeed all of Queen are.

One of the world's greats – Brian May (Knighthood please ma'am asap.)

The wonderful Brian May

HAPPY DAYS

The good, the bad, and the gormless

I truly believe that if you can focus on one thing which you love to bits and are totally passionate about, that this can be a great and effective way to short-circuit any negative feelings brought on by life's many pinhead critics.

Mine was music and art.

However, it does take some strong willpower and this can be in short supply after a thoughtless comment or snide remark brings you crashing down to the ground. My way around this was to write everything down the way I saw it. I make my own clothes, create my own designs, write my own songs.

By doing this you are releasing the growing tensions which can bring on your own anxiety, devastation and eventually deep depression.

One of my major upsets began in the early seventies when Greek coffee bars suddenly started blatantly advertising prejudice and prejudgemental intolerance with banners stating their policy of:

NO LONG HAIR

I remember being deeply offended by all this and thinking, "What's going on?" Yet to question their policy was met by sheer malice and bitter rudeness. Now I've always had a passion for the evolution of trends and fashion – this is my whole world.

Our early coffee bars in the West End of London spawned such fabulous artists as Cliff Richard, Tommy Steele and many others. And in America, where the great coffee bar culture of the fifties and sixties evolved, they belonged to the kids – keeping them safe, away from trouble, and bought everyone together to meet up and have fun under a backdrop of Elvis Presley, Eddie Cochran, Buddy Holly and the rest – as typified by TV's "Happy Days" show.

Guitars, beehive hairdo's, Bobby sox, T-Birds, pickup trucks, and the Ford Mustang – incredible! Then to have to witness these greasy-haired, blinkered individuals with their "NO LONG HAIR" posters planted all down the High Street was just too much to take.

And to put up with this shit after feeling so proud of our sixties London Scene, along with Carnaby Street, the fashions of Paris, plus the wonderful music of The Kinks, The Who, The Small Faces, Mama Cass, Jimi Hendrix, Janis Joplin and all the many others…

Our British flag meant so much all over the world. The world in which we'd won the World Cup and had all this positive energy – from the Mini Cooper S to pop stars riding around in Rolls Royces – it was great fun!

Then these foreign attempts at misery and social segregation…

I remember thinking that soon there would be dim, gormless bouncers in every pub doorway telling us what we can and can't wear. So came "NO LONG HAIR" in our High Streets!

Well, here are some suggestions for them: *No modern fashions*, *No English or

British*, *No Looking Good*, *Slimy, Greasy, Hairy-chested Medallion-wearing Men Only*, *No Women*, *No Feminine Men*, *Big Oily 'Taches* (like mummy's), *No Poufs, Coloured Hair or Men in Nail Varnish.*

"NO LONG HAIR" in Britain – you're having a laugh. Get back home to Shitsville with your duff coffee and Brylcreem.

"You don't have to be Mr Macho Man – women aren't like this which is why they make better drivers! (Stevie Ze)

Let us remain untampered with and free to express ourselves!

My beautiful people:

Cross-dressers, *Trans-sexuals*, *Gay and Lesbian Pride of Britain*, *High Street and Alternative Fashion*, *Same-sex marriage*, *Dedicated Followers of Fashion*.

Well, this is the west and we also have… Mods, Rockers, Punks, Rappers, Animal Lovers, Dreadlock bleach-blonde Ice Cream Smiles…

All stood together on the Murder Mile!

PRETTY IN THE CITY

In the City

Lookin' prissi

Dressed a little

Like a Queen

With a cross

On her head

Against the

Media machine

She smiles

Like a reptile

With diamond

Studded claws

As she files her nails

Outside the House of Lords

And sometimes people
Start pushing you around
Sometimes they all
Act like fools

Be it a Rolling Stone
Riding in a pink Cadillac
While they bitch
About the price of fuel

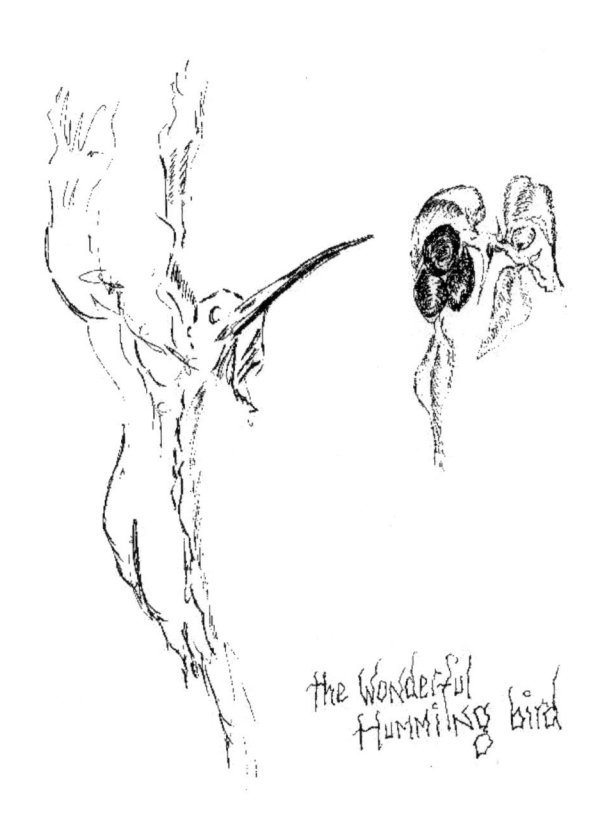

the Wonderful Humming bird

SATURDAY SCREAMERS

Well my darlings, it's the weekend again and the Saturday screamers are filling up at their local drinking dives on weak lager, gin and diet fibre – each accompanied by two or three kids from previous vile encounters.

Yes folks, complete with shaved heads, fat arses and revolting hairy tits hanging right down to the floor. Leggings and fave football shirts, adorned of course. These are the REAL great unwashed as Churchill described.

Human garbage bins in full football strip surrounded by their big fat kids - and they have more kids than teeth, it seems - all burping up pop and crisps whilst smelling of unwashed backsides, as their parents get tanked up before the footy results at five pm! Then it's outside for the old e-cig with mighty clouds of vapour for a gossip consisting of total bollocks and talent shows.

Inside, a group of hopeless tribute acts perform in between the karaoke clowns and bingo vomit.

"Beam me up Scotty!"

Yes, welcome to the Saturday and Sunday cabaret element inside their crass bubble of pub culture.

What wonderful and intellectually stimulating fun to be had by all!!

And at the end of the day they will all stagger home, burping and farting and spewing up every few yards, with kebab and chips in hand 'til they eventually reach home to undoubtable copulate once again like a well-oiled chav production line! "More kids?" And all this misery for the sake of a shag!

Perhaps they should hold a "Guess who's kid it'll be this year" contest.

New Hot News !!

Grand Dad

"Chav Mania" has arrived

"Chav Mania is fun... fun for all the family with big cash prizes – be won every nine months when you play......

Guess Who's Kid it is?

the popular new pub quiz sweeping the nation !!

First Prize: Your own personalised spitoon!

The bad, the worse, & the stupid...

Punk is Just Rubbish

Foundry Worker Sheffield Way

and as the great unwashed gather around their local watering hole of bullshit and skittles, we must surely ask ourselves about the evolutionary progress of the human being - we've devised and built the most sophisticated longe-range communication systems, plus the knowledge to put a man on the moon - yet still find amusement in drawing each other's private parts on bog walls!

Gosh, wiff, niff, QUICK,..... BINGO IS ON!!!, whaaa, stench, waft

I AM AN OWL

I am a little Owl
I toot n' hoot n' howl
Just like the Lion Roars
but they stay on the floor

I can see in flight
through out the night
with big sharp eyes
so shiny bright

I gaze in seach
of moon lit glades
watch dawn aproach
across the graves

Church Mice scurry
from new sun rise,
before they are caught
in bright sunshine

When flys + Moths + Mice + Voles
will disapear
down little holes
they must be careful
I don't see them
or for my dinner
I may eat them !!!

My baby Owl

so hide in safety
beneath the flowers
while I patrol
these Mid-Night hours

this little Eagle
so unfolds
with wealth of selth
from ages old

to glide & skim
the ground so fast
before the due forms
upon the grass

I am but such
a little Owl
yet full of life
& standing Proud

BOB IN A BOTTLE

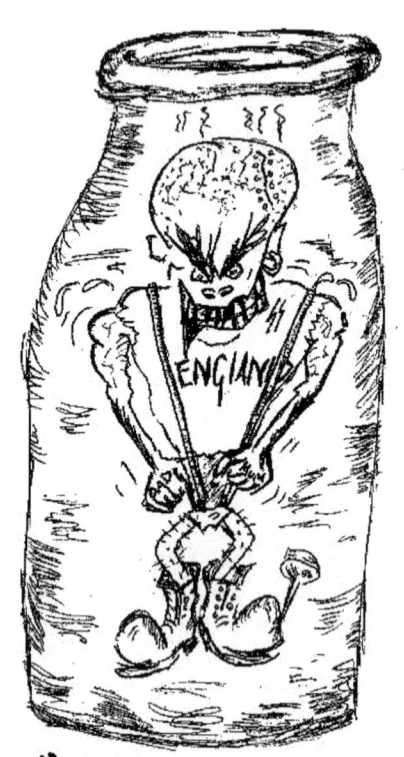

"Bob in a Bottle"
this seathing, heaving, hating, self opinion-
-ated mess can be found in almost all
urban areas,
everyone must enevitably know one,
yes, this primative know all is commonly
found in most karioki pubs, working mens
clubs and chip shops across the land.

Desperate Pam

as is Mrs Shite brain,..... Yes, "Mrs Bottle" is well versed in condoms and bingo,. Although the birth control aspect seems to have avoided her sweaty Arse so far!!!

Bob in a bottle also has a shaved head but with nothing inside it. His many inhibitions are all bottled up inside him and he looks like a tattooed pink ape without fur. In fact, big hardman homophobic Bob and the 'Love Island' plastic luvvy-duvvies he dates ARE apes (with all due respect to real apes).

Welcome to Suburbia!

With an average of eleven kids from their previous ape encounters their lives free-base in non-thought. And their horrendous kids – each looking like little red satellite dishes stuffed full of pork scratchings and pop, burping as loudly as possible in a usual apprentice yob manner, spitting every few seconds, while smelling of raw minced meat and too much daytime TV.

The atmosphere in their local pub must be like a free for all ape gang-bang – a frenzy of bullshit and duff empty plans of nowhereness – as they get ever more and more excited until closing time.

And these are the creatures who have the affront to call me "Pink-haired freak," amongst many other abusive comments!

WONDERFUL!

~ ~ ~ ~ ~ ~

An iconic God is born

But a lethargic lost lamb

Yet rises from the abyss

To make life their insistence

Stevie Ze

SLADE

If you go onto my website StevieZeSuicide.com and into the 'Video' section, you will find an interview I did a few years ago now with one of my all-time favourite and influential bands... Slade. I talked at length with drummer Don Powell and guitarist Dave Hill – who are still taking the band on the road to this day!

Actually, they were by far the biggest influence on me. They banished the bores and defied their critics – the bigheads, the know-alls, and the posh snob rock cissy-poo's. And what they taught me was how to entertain! The dressing up, the stage presence, and most of all, the audience participation.

I mean – look at The Spice Girls, how brilliantly they were put together they were, a marketing phenomenon, both looking and sounding great, with each individual girl possessing their own star power – and thus appealing to every teen in the land.

Girl power had arrived! Plus star power at its very best.

With Slade I also admired Sweet, T Rex, and of course the most androgynous superstar of all time, David Bowie as Ziggy Stardust with his Spiders from Mars. This all led me later to Marilyn Manson and Lady GaGa, but first…

The best was yet to come in the shape of the fabulous Punk Rock – my kind of music! That was ours, you know, it belonged to the people, the real people, and totally eliminating the elite musicians of local 'go nowhere' snobbery.

Even at school I always took note of the fashion statements of sixties London – The Kinks, The Who, and The Small Faces, all with their superb hair styles. Dave Davies with his red Gibson Flying V, Jagger's flamboyant stage presence, the military look of Carnaby Street jackets worn by my hero Jimi Hendrix. Mary Quant dresses, tops and mini skirts, hipsters, and above all the MUSIC, the FABULOUS MUSIC!

Now – in these later times – that early education shines through now as I listen to the great music of today. Whilst driving this year, I heard a brand new song on the radio called 'Dear Darling,' written and performed by Ollie Murrs and I had to stop the car to listen to this masterpiece of writing skill. I was reduced to tears of joy by this man – who was he?

I remained in my car for quite a while as I contemplated all the feeling that had gone into the work, and I remembered all those who had told me:

"You can't do this."

"You can't do that."

"You can't do anything."

But you can when you put your mind to it – and don't let ANYONE put you off! Remember NO-ONE has that right over your life.

Each of you are a beautiful rainbow of life, and life belongs to that very special you. The great music of today is quite unsurpassed by its wonderful content.

John Legend's 'All of Me,' written by Will.I.Am – a seriously amazing genius song from amazingly genius artists. We have reached a peak intelligence like never before, with such fabulous artists like KT Tunstall, Paloma Faith, Lady GaGa, Kaiser Chiefs,

Ed Sheeran, George Ezra, Will.I.Am... I feel I could go on for ever. And all spawned from an exciting new era in entertainment!

From my influences during the nineties, such as Marilyn Manson, Guns 'n' Roses, and many more to The Killers, Biffy Clyro, The Foo Fighters and Greenday, it all seems to have got better and better.

BBC Radio 2's dj's creating great listening and great fun – friendly fun. We have Zoe Ball, Steve Wright, Michael Ball, Johnny Walker, Dermot O'Leary and Craig David – all with a knowledge and love of their music and possessing total respect for what is happening today!

No nasties here!

Perhaps there is no room for the old-fashioned nasties anymore? Just great friendly fun for a planet that surely needs it!

So I thank you Slade for bringing us sheer entertainment value – and such blisteringly fun tunes! And for helping to influence and shape the future of modern entertainment.

To Noddy Holder, Dave Hill, Don Powell, and Jimmy Lea – knighthoods all round please ma-am!

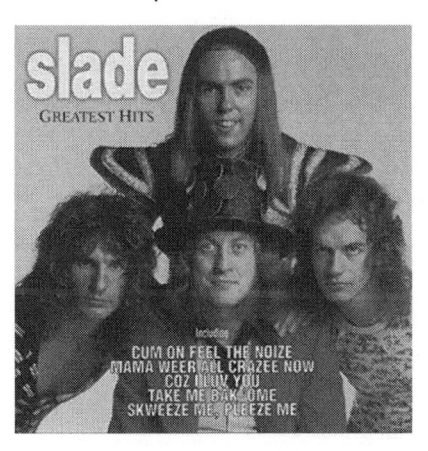

PAPARAZZI BABES

Femme fatales and suicidal rides

For heroes are below zero and as cold as ice

Lady GaGa trips the light fantastique

Chic and so unique

She is Paradise

Dreadlock bleach blonde ice cream smiles

In lizard leather plastic boots

Nothing's ever what it seems

So excuse me while I bleach my roots

Here's another singer from a soap box romance

With an enigmatic smile of reality TV

Paparazzi babes in kaleidoscope lipstick

Be careful what you eat or you'll never stay thin

SMELL THE ART

Smell the art as movement grows

As tears subside and beauty glows

Smell the art that takes your breath

The leaves lethargic moments blessed

Embrace the art's romantic splendour

And all the wonders draped in gender

Testing boundaries proud and strong

For this is a place where I belong

be a Rainbow

DAVID JOHN EARL

David John Earl is a major airbrush artist and a legend in his profession – simply the best!

Not only that, he is the most fabulous guitarist and performer on stage. I wasn't surprised to find out that he had grown up watching our very own Nicky Garrett from UK Subs!.

Check out his spectacular band 'Dogsflesh; and you'll see what I mean! Good man, David John Earl – you're a true star and a friend!

David John Earl – airbrush genius… pretty hot guitarist, too!

I AM A WORM

My God

I am a worm
and I wriggle round
+ squirm
but we protect your Earth
+ purify the dirt

I'll dig deep down
to enrich my soul
Avoiding birds
who can swallow me whole

We make a garden thrive
oh it's great to be alive
without us here
your plants won't grow
We are the engineers down below

So I am just as usefull too
for bringing all this life to you!!
+ in the engine room
where no one goes
beneath the flower beds
new life glows

FROM A PRIESTESS TO A STAR

Sable has a laser-covered

Cadillac to ride

Cruised it down to Hollywood

With stardust in her eyes

Twenty flight rock and Johnny's

Got himself a band

Slips into an ego

With a bottle close at hand

The billion dollar babies out of school

Just like the lizard hero from a space invasion

Playing rock and roll guitar

From a priestess to a star

Snow White is just a

Candy-covered junkie on the slide

Struts her stuff on Broadway
In amphetamine disguise

So juicy in her movies
With a six-gun in her hand
While Paul is Sergeant Pepper's
Lonely Hearts Club Band

Marc is now a 22nd Century boy
Born to boogie like a floozie
He's a mean mistreater
Playing rock and roll guitar
From a priestess to a star

Joanna Jett's a superstar
Much more than just a girl
Who's smile can light the universe
And brighten up the world

GaGa is so beautifully
Focussed on romance
While Johnny sings Imagine
If we all give peace a chance

Barbie's got a flick knife and a string of pearls

Now she gets her kicks as Queen Bitch

Playing rock and roll guitar

From a priestess to a star.

Lady Suicide

HOUNDS OF HELL

As I drive away from this abyss
Encouraged by the Devil's wish
And blaze a trail, the hounds of Hell
Within me rise to kiss and tell

An inevitable poignancy to my anger
How revenge tastes sweet in shades of languor

Now pain and hurt may soon subside
And release my playful peace of mind

Expel those vicious plagued vendettas
Replace with hope and all that matters

Embrace the love so long denied
So lost when dogs of war collide

THE GREAT LOCAL NUMPTY SWINDLE - PART 1

The gripping success story of an unlikely rock star surrounded by sheer muck-encrusted amateurs.

Disclaimer: Any resemblance to any persons past or present is purely coincidental – or a figment of your own paranoia!

Stevie ZeSuicide

Reginald Humphrey Shingles Gaspipe Blenkinsop Blair Reasonable Dick is a book-smeller, part-time tiddlywink champion and well-versed camel expert. Well-known for sniffing trees, Reggie's not married but lives with his mother who he feeds on raw bacon, and keeps under the stairs with a dead rabbit and a blue flask that his uncle brought him back from Spain.

Now Reggie knows a local MP called Maurice with whom he plans to build a submarine – he loves the smell of

Maurice's books as well as his oil or petrol soaked underpants. He also enjoys playing naked dominos once a month with the local parish councillors Guild of Rabbit Ticklers from the bare-arsed bird watchers club nearby. These twitchers often meet in a little hut in the woods where they all pull their underpants right up tight and watch the little birdies with the pale cheeks of their bare arses and their little dickies showing. Nice!

Back at home, however, Reggie pours himself a rather large sherry in his favourite Ollie Murrs cup and slips into his very special rubber nurses outfit and puts his new Phil Collins album on. He relaxes into his Cliff Richard's Summer Holiday bean bag.

He gazes at the signed photo of Tom Jones's bum hole hanging on the wall and settles down to read his copy of the new book – an autobiography by the enigmatic Les McKeown called, simply and ironically, 'Penis.'

Reggie admires Phil 'Funboy' Collins' head so much he has a strong urge to make mad passionate love to it! He often wonders if Mr Collins got that hairstyle idea from a Playboy centrefold

With 'laugh a second' Collins now warbling through yet another tedious 'unlucky in love' requiem mass, and with Mother screaming "Bacon! Bacon!" as the mice throw themselves mercilessly into the traps beneath the stairs, he drifts away into a totally uneventful, boredom induced, coma.

Nelly 'No Knickers' fries a sausage or two for a banquet on behalf of the local bare-arsed society gathering Rotary Club gang of upper to middle class bird watchers spectacular abortions Ltd.

Tonight's show stars a Kim Jon Un tribute act performing Bing Crosby favourites on behalf of the Liberal Democrats, while the Big Hard Biker Twins dance away to 'Last Christmas' by 'Wham'.

Plus: comedy tricks from Bay City Rollers singer Les McKeown – as the rude and insulting Butlins favourite will perform naked Scotty boy acrobatics – then try to sing songs he has written all by himself without people laughing.

Reggie begins to dream of becoming a rock star in a perfect suburban environment where he can join the local Rotary Club and mingle with two-faced musical drips and Christian pre-judgemental church mice over tea and Jesus cocaine cake.

His prayers and dreams were about to be answered – in the form of underwater promoter and well-known constant small fry music liar, Fish Criminal, with his assistant, Pipe, secretary Pool of Sick, and record label who have such fabulous artists as... Well, NONE, actually! Together they formed Bumhole Records after seeing Tom's big signed picture on Reggie's wall.

The hairy grey bum-holed one stands as an inspiration to any new artist – but beware, Fish, you have a rival also on the amateur local muffin scene

WELCOME TO: The Great Local Numpty Swindle!

Starring Fish Criminal, assistant Pipe, Secretary Pool of Sick

Co-starring the Flightie Pa Pa's boogie triers and singing, bricklaying, overnight sensation that is… Bubble Uppa Ladder Skinskull and his band, guitarist Blistering Paddleboat Pete, Plumbing Zappo Tinylegs.

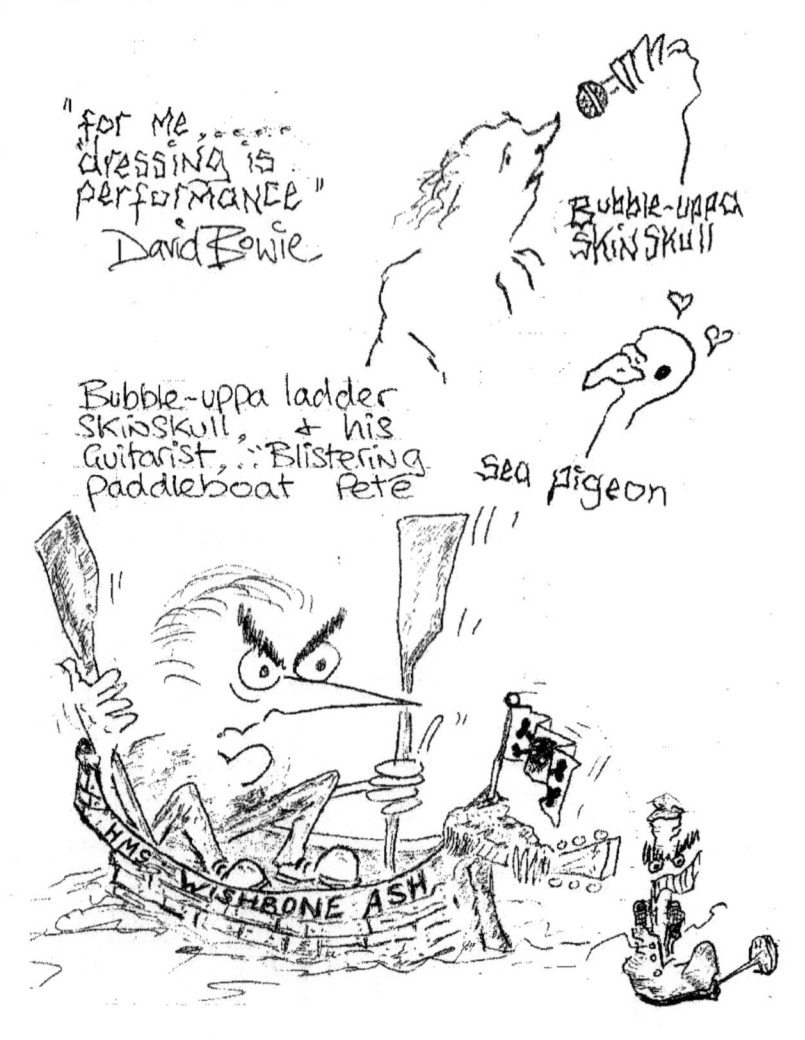

So exactly who were these frightie-nightie pantyhose boys anyway? Well, true Wild West heroes, these boys, but unfortunately only rockers on a weekend –just like the Saturday night screamers, and like so many, only if allowed by their wives of bosses, or mummy and daddy, whatever, whatever, whatever.

So there they were, soon to be chewed up and spat out by a control mad freaky beaked one. Well, let's not forget that it was Blistering Paddleboat Pete who once referred to all musicians as freeloaders. Maybe they deserved what they got.

Yes, it's a struggle Paddleboat, but not everyone is scared shitless like YOU! And not everyone is a freeloader! You know, sometimes I wonder why on earth these types are even in bands in the first place? Is it ego, fame, sex, showing off… or what?

And so says the Blistering knowall: Bloody damned freeloaders. Bash them – bash them all! Bash everything!

These bands probably had guys who had all been at school together and remain in their flock forever, like sheep. They will all live within a ten mile radius of each other until the day they die – objective and frightened by difference and as safe as houses, they will all stick together. But don't just sit and criticise or come near me with your little hobby – I simply don't care any more.

"See how they run like pigs from a gun, see how they shy."

John Lennon

"I'm not a slave to a God that doesn't exist

I'm not a slave to a world that doesn't give a shit."

Marilyn Manson

ENTER: Crispy Lip – the local wrecking ball beak.

Just check out that beak of deceit. However, back in Cretinville, final resting place of Dick Turpin, Crispy Lip has found –the Flighty hopeless gits of fear. This is a band clearly trapped in Man at C & A. A typically useless commodity of glory boys pretending, and so afraid to ever leave their little village – yet a perfect vehicle for the Beak of deceit.

It was, of course, the Crispy Lipped Wrecking Ball liar's idea of Bubble Uppa Ladder Skinskull and the Builder Snowmen as the new name for this band of brown bootie boys, formerly known as Flights of Fear. Crispy Lip, however, wants much more than just this. He wants Bumhole Records too, but will have to get around Fish first for that one.

Sea Pigeon and Mountain Pig appear by courtesy of Fart Gizza Clue Huge Backsides Model Agency.

Secretary Pool of Sick takes up the story…

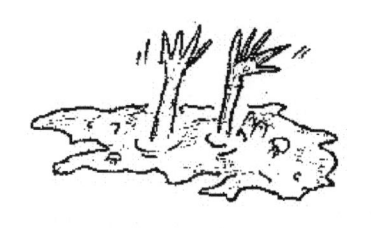

"We decided to sign Reggie to the Bumhole Record label and create a star called Popcorn Dick with, hopefully, an original song from somewhere. That's when we found Crispy Lip, known as Wrecking Ball beak, as he has a kind of funny crispy beak. We found him right here in Whitby, selling musical kippers and goldfish as Koi carp from Tom Petty's garden pond in LA for EMI. Lucky old us! Turning our back for a second wasn't wise, but Fish Criminal knows how to deal and watch out for daggers so we were okay as the beak grinned back at us through deep cadaver dead eyes that said nothing.

"For Popcorn Dick he gave us a song called 'Overnight Sensation' but we soon discovered that The Bay City Rollers had already written that one in the shape of 'Summerlove Sensation' which Crispy Lip had blatantly copied. We decided to release something else instead as a single.

"When Crispy Lip got a sniff of this he ran in with his voice of an angel - of course, well known musical muffin Bubble Uppa - grabbed Fish dramatically in his beak and threatened Fish Criminal as *he* wants everything to own for *himself...* NOW!

"He demands, "Use my song for Popcorn Dick!" Fish replies, "But 'Overnight Sensation' is a one hundred percent rip-off! True, very true!

"Crispy's increasingly weird beak starts to curl up. It's now clear that an upset spoilt Crispy can be a tricky Dicky son of a plantpot when he wants! You see, he has a band already called The Flightie Travel Sick Hobo Cretins, fronted by his very own 'monkey on a stick' karaoke champion and wood pigeon fancier Bubble Uppa Ladder Skinskull... A stonemason by trade, just like daddy

Skinskull, who's said to have built Yorkminster's toilet seats out of banana skins. Pity he didn't make any to put on his head!

"Crispy's next musical abortion 'Cattle Grid Coma' is all about himself, completely about himself, and he OWNS it ALL! Even boasting owning an old toilet roll once used by Tom Petty. He insists the band The Flighty Sausage Boys must now be called The Skinskulls and this name shall belong to him and him alone. From now on he will write ALL the songs, and He will take ALL the money! This is now HIS band and they will do as they're told!

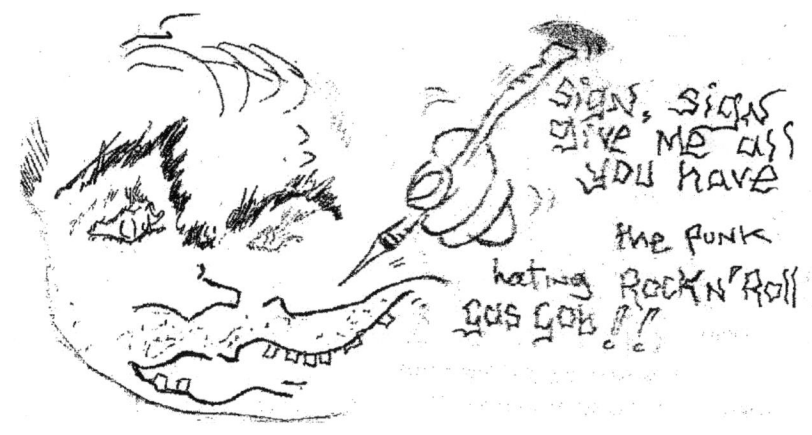

"Suddenly a happy local band were in trouble! They had a 'music tick.'

"As Picasso said – it's not what you steal, it's how you use it!"

David Bowie

Meanwhile Reggie becomes increasingly tired of being Popcorn Dick on Bumhole Records, suffering duff songs from Crispy which could have come from a kipper farm. So Reggie records Marilyn Manson songs and tells no-one. He films videos and shows and tells no-one. And, as his new profile builds into something special, he quietly moves on and in for the kill.

Changing his name to Skeletal Bacteria he teams up with Goth Prince of Death keyboard player Vue X Monroe. This is the Vue X with a reputation for stalking the dead in cemeteries across the world. Suddenly Reggie's career is finally rescued by the Prince of Death himself. The demonic producer/composer seemed to be sent as a gift from the Earth's central core – straight from Hell, if you like – and the keyboard demon Vue X Monroe took Reggie, as Skeletal Bacteria, under his wing and has, at last, given him tracks of professional quality.

No bullshit from this man!

Vue X Monroe

Celebrations were now in in order at Skeletal's success. His father expresses his pride.

"My son is now an icon thanks to Vue X Monroe. I am very proud."

Sir Cyril Belcher MBE

Reggie's new recordings under Vue X's supervision are a true success story as they celebrate with brand new songs. Skeletal Bacteria has at last arrived. A star is born.

As The Flighties sink further down in their muddy brown builder thug boots to the crass oblivion caused by their own inevitable blandness. Reggie becomes his own alter ego within this re-invention and finds new strength within himself. Then Fish Criminal has a great idea… we'll have Pool of Sick on our record label. She will be Atomic Vomit Girl – and kept a million light years away from Crispy Lip! So they release a Vue X Monroe song called Sisters of Satan and it is a great triumph for them all.

And so she has arrived, everyone is celebrating and so happy. Atomic Vomit Girl is a success thanks mostly to the brilliant Vue X Monroe and his demonic keyboards, and a good time is had by all. It's a noise revolution, baby!

Pool of Sick becomes Atomic Vomit Girl

Fish also signs Suzi Sledgehammer to his label. Good times!

Around the same time Fishy also discovers and signs a new girl group called Electric Witch and the Babe Squad. Super loud and unafraid they blend perfectly with wonderful chaos as proper artists should do. With the added bonus of death keyboard genius Vue X Monroe, the man said to be responsible for many fresh grave robberies. Narcissistically loud as fuck and unstoppably sick!

(top)Electric Witch, Barbi Witch, Sinister Witch, Gay Witch

(below) Pretty Witch

By now Crispy's curly lip falls to the floor as he stands in the cold with just a box of kippers.

So, for new artists it is springtime... the frightened safety brigade of inhibitions are no longer needed and the priests hang on hooks.

Part 2 – The Conclusion of Vortex – coming soon!

"Being a star is the only thing I do that doesn't bore me."

David Bowie

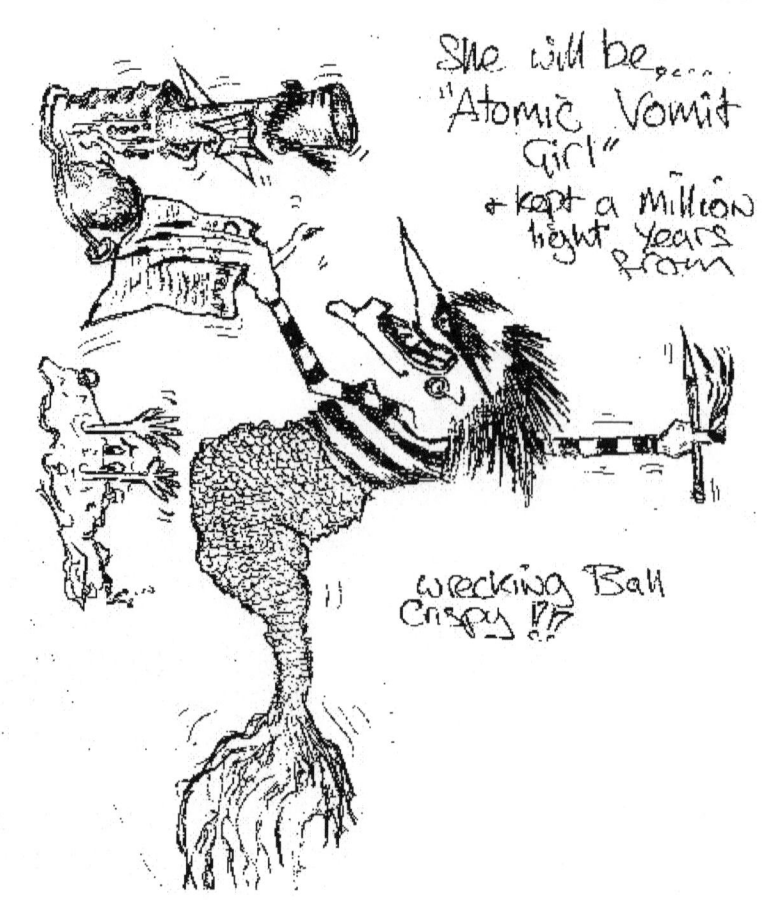

"I was talking to myself – but no-one's home!"

Axl Rose

On finding out, Crispy's lip twists so far around his gob that his teeth stick out of the back of his big head! "I wanna write. I wanna write," is all he cries until his tears run down his back, as his head now spins around like a demented top. "Help me, help me. I write everything. I must be one of the Beatles, the twisted big-gobbed one. I must be!"

"I never really hated any one true God

but the God of the people I hated."

Marilyn Manson

EPILOGUE:

Will punk rock finally burst Crispy's bubble?

Will Paddleboat 'Know-All" finally find happiness out on the ocean?

Will Bubble Uppa Ladder Skinskull ever reach the top of his ladder and marry a wood pigeon with an egg ready to hatch?

Meanwhile Skeletal Bacteria becomes more and more famous with Atomic Vomit Girl – and Suzy Sledgehammer is touring the world.

* DON'T MISS *

THE GREAT NUMPTI SWINDLE PART 2

THE CONCLUSION OF VORTEX

Pastel Ghetto
stole a Rock n' Roll guitar
became a Rock n' Roll star
plays it sick, loud, insane
silver bullets
through your brain
wild trash beauty
who is next
for your lavish pure
sadistic sex

Pastel Ghetto

"my breasts are of FiFi Darling and Belong to No-One."

Pastel Ghetto

FUCK PIGS OF NONSENSE

If sick means piss

It affects your throat

Watch them choke and gloat

With senseless dopes

Listening to their constant nonsense

Wildebeests of zero conscience

The shite within their factory walls

Readers of garbage – know-it-alls

Shit, sick, fuck pigs

Fucking balls

Can make life hell

'Til Heaven calls

When Heaven calls

I'll be miles away

So I don't have to face

Another day

Of cackling plastic

Scrotum-coated Billy-Bongs

Shouting their might

While smelling of shite

I will be gone, by God

Away with the fairies

From beer thugs and insults

And beefcake contraries

THE GREAT LOCAL NUMPTY SWINDLE - PART 2

The conclusion of Vortex

After finding a better class of musical enterprise with no more aerial bending stomach churning pus bollox, Reginald Shinglelegs Blenkinsop becomes a superstar hero called 'Skeletal Bacteria' with a fabulous debut album titles 'Lick me to death over a nice hot tin of soup.'

Plus a brand new single released from the album, entitled 'Kiss me Where it Smells by the Duck Pond, Honey Babe.' All written by Reggie himself. Also Vue X Monroe gave him 'London Vampire' and 'Legacy of the Terminator' which can be viewed on YouTube,

This was all recorded, of course, as soon as he was as far away as possible from musical dictator Crispy Lip, or Beak of the Week Wrecking Ball, as he is known.

And all a million light years from the Genesis, Wishbone Ash style of soft rock stinkers of the big headed, spoilt boy local bay window Doobie Brothers twat set!

Yes, Reginald, our Sketelal Bacteria star now, lives in well domestic splendour, with former MP Maurice wearing his tight rubber suit in their new submarine names 'Rose Marie' after a really drearily dreadful song he was once sent when he was singing as Popcorn Dick.

Maurice just loves dancing to Skeletal music – 'Death in the City' being his favourite written by the demon of Satan himself, Vue X Monroe for Atomic Vomit Girl.

They cosily settle down to watch their favourite movie – 'War Tortoise.' Set on the coast during World War 2, Tortoise Commander Pumping Adda-Gas is sent over to obtain vital secrets from Adolf Hitler disguised as a German helmet. But, on the way home he falls in love with a European plant pot called Daisy and they start a family of little plant pots all called Kevin.

Meanwhile, up and down his hapless ladder travels Skinskull, watched closely by Sea Pigeon, and followed around by a putrid, super-duper, 'done-fuck-all,' yet self-appointed music critic and clothes-designing liar, now holiday chalet bog cleaner, Julian Potato-Brain. He is almost completely invisible to the naked human eye except for his bucket of soapy water and cloth – just like so many bland Herberts who are all dressed the same as each other.

Now, having been a top bog bloke, and knitting specialist to the ignorant smelly obsessed scrotums of barrel bottom City, here he sits like a very proud, crab-like obstacle indeed. What a sight! Yuk!

Being locked down and forever in dead end street now seemed quite imminent for the softie rock boys in brown wellies... Then suddenly, a new musical development for the Bubble Uppas.

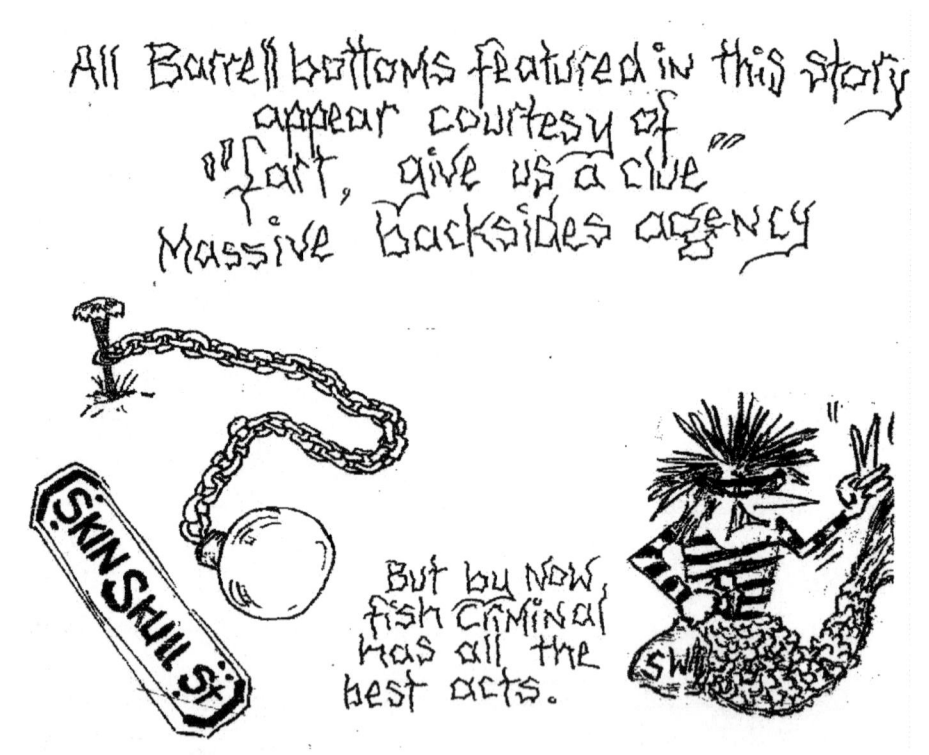

All Barrel bottoms featured in this story appear courtesy of "Tart, give us a clue" Massive Backsides agency

But by now, fish Criminal has all the best acts.

Yes, the shitey flighty brown-booted muffin boys are all sat together down the pub, busily picking each other's noses, just like all apes do, when in slithers Crispy Lip himself, beak a-flapping left to right like an epileptic flag in a gale.

A frightened fireplace boy, covered in cement dust, stands up as Crispy Lip reveals that his dumpling-shaped counterpart, Plastic Spastic Murphy, from down South, has found 30K – that's probably kippers – to throw at the pub band. The terrified stone mason bursts into tears of joy. "Please can we re-release my 'Overnight Sensation' – and I need some more flares to wear..."

But the Lip needs a house and the Lip needs a car, in fact the Lip wants everything he can get his slippery, twisted flippers on!

Meanwhile Blistering Paddleboat Pete, super hard man 'know it all' and Brain of Britain, is now clearly head of York's Sheep Brigade, a bunch of joined at the hip Neanderthals, and is taking freeloading professional musicians (as the shallow builder calls us all) very seriously indeed as an excuse for his own lack of balls which always stopped him even trying for himself... enjoy your own blank brain!

Of course Crispy Lip now made a beeline for any cash that was around. Eagerly booking a remote farmhouse in Scotland for his well-trained, yet terrified, turkeys, the mighty flighty nightie, non-fashion, papa's namby-pamby Nancy boy sausage-munchers, where they could rehearse all his dreadfully dull and dismal songs.

Yet the band were never destined to see even one kipper! And this folks is the swindle. One snowy night a noise was heard outside, and next morning there were human footprints in the snow. Could this have been Crispy's mysterious 'kippers' arriving? Meant for the band, from Plastic Spastic Murphy con man via a carrier sheep wearing cowboy boots.

The farmhouse was never paid for. (Sounds about right!) Crispy Lip the Beak fled. Last seen riding away on a stolen donkey with what appeared to be a little 'Beatles' rucksack on his back.

'RIDE CREEPO, RIDE!'

The Crispy Lip then tries to move in on Atomic Vomit Girl and Suzy Sledgehammer as he has nothing of his own – but is met by a very angry Fish who strangles the creep almost to oblivion.

His Lip quivered but wasn't letting go. He continued to lie through those crooked teeth of his, whilst filling up his vast greedy beak with more local band booty, for he needs Murphy's kipper donation for a brand new act to ruin – as finally the super-duper, flighty-nightie, clueless, sheep-like, big-headed flock of goats had run back to the building site oblivion, where they all clearly belong, and should never have tried to leave in the first place!

"Stay away from my artists parasite twisted gob..."

Now Crispy Lip Wrecking Ball of Deceit has a new act called 'Pop turns to Dog Business.' A similar mess to his last band, The Little Arseholes, who flopped into his invisible black hole abyss, which is safe, nothingness oblivion.

Well, as we all know, Crispy Lip never made it to Top of the Pops. However, over in Belgium – yes in BELGIUM! – apparently top

rock and roll performer, known as the Belgian Beaker is none other than Crispy Lip himself!! This is also where he claims to have written 'A Hard Day's Night' and 'Help.' Plus, according to himself, he is a massive star who tours alone by train and is mobbed by screaming fans wherever he goes.

Yes – ladies and gentlemen – this is the Belgian Beaker, who, by the way, no-one else seems to have ever heard of! Anyway, he looks a right cunt with a quiff!

Back in York Admiral Paddleboat Pete, who calls all us real musicians freeloaders, threatens the world – well, York, actually – with his hard man stance and hatred of professional musicians.

Bubble Uppa Skinskull is also around here somewhere and is now expecting his first egg with Sea Pigeon!

Bubble-Uppa Relaxes "Do you fancy a round of Karioke-egg tennis my love of sea pigeon?" "Oh yes my darling and I am now with egg"

This is a true horror story, yet so common. Plus a warning of just what type of turkeys are out there – so BEWARE!

All the users, accusers, the triers and flyers, all the robbers and knobbers and twisted elite, the fakes and the flakes, all the liars and the cheats, the blood-sucking gobbies and disintegration freaks. All the stealers and wheelers, dealers and thieves, human energy vampires in empires of greed, monkey see monkey do tribute disasters, hate-filled parasitic negatives and bastards. Two-faced bitch slappers and rappers, monkey-brained musical tics and all-time meddlers, bullshit producers and bigheads who bitch.

I'm sitting in a downtown bar (the usual old shite hole) filled with the ghosts of past musical hopelessness, the Saturday night screamers, and the sort of place you find human vultures. There's a dull, dross juke box in the corner playing all the bland garbage it possibly can – and there's chicken wire across the tiny stage to protect cover bands from certain death by a tiny audience who know Jack shit about anything at all – especially music! "No alternatives here," say the landlords.

"No Alternatives here" say the landlords,....

So: dance, dance, dance little Nazi's

Karaoki yourselves to death

At the bar the umbilically connected Siamese sheep gather around to exchange their daily bullshit. All locked together for safety in numbers... the Paddleboats and builders and bog cleaners all become super self-satisfied but resentful unto death, obsessing over old fireplaces, and crying into their beers with their muddy, dust-covered thug boots and grey hair thinning by the second, about what would have been "if only they'd been given the chance!"

Of course, it's everyone else's fault – not their own!

Crispy's brand new live act is just as terrifically crass as his usual garbage. Ex-Little Arseholes frontman, Toby Toilet-Seat, is supporting his new band – a seriously undangerous, no-ideas formula, sheer non-excitement forming, backward looking, usual safe, muck-encrusted mess called 'Crispy and the Muffins'.

At the same time Skeletal Bacteria and Atomic Vomit Girl are far way, touring the world and doing very well away from Crispy Lip, thank you!

Fish Criminal still operates today – in a very small way – as does Crispy Gob, who is now very rarely even seen. As they failed to ever be professionals or achieve a hit, they all hide away in the shadows – so sad really!

On a higher note, sexy Atomic Vomit Girl married Sexy Suzy Sledgehammer, whilst the highly successful Reggie 'Skeletal Bacteria' finally tied the knot with his beloved Maurice in their luxury submarine.

Pipe threw himself back into the sea while Sea Pigeon gave birth to a big headed, heavy metal bass nobody, called 'Dross' who apparently is a huge superstar in Finland with his little Yorkie outfit called 'The Farters.'

Bubble Uppa and Mad Paddleboat Pete found fame as tinned meat-based products in supermarket bargain bins.

I'm so pleased to be away from all this local bullshit crowd. I walked out without looking back at them, knowing that things can never change in Cretinville!

"Bop Bop!!"

Biff Biff

Kirk Kill

Mad Pete the Blistering Paddle Boat

Top Leader of the Rabbit Brigade Sheep gang!!!! of arse smellers Ltd.

"Three" "Ted know" Free Loaders

"Stop" all this silly Guitar-ness

Mad PADDLEBOAT PETE!!!!
undisputable know all,....

MAD paddleboat freeloader hater says,....

"I am boatMAN and hate Losers" kill him

Kill xhem ALL!!!

↓ GET A PROPER JOB Like Me "Paddleboat"

shite old then got a stupid fireplace to obsess over & impress the silver headed sadds of bland-ness

185

YES, you will enjoy this
bright + wonderful new act!
as they sail through a
Repertoire of Crispy songs
+ covers !?!?
Even more exciting than a
George Formby tribute or a
Bernard Manning show
.... "don't Miss"...
ooh total snot release babes'
Crispy lip
Crispy + the Muffins
Bog face
moonshine pig muck
Bog face

the END

I watched the voice of an angel destroyed by a vulture

I saw a great band devoured by a user.

Stevie Ze

From 'Rage of a Vixen'

RAGE OF A VIXEN

I watched the voice of an angel

Devoured by a vulture

A once great rock band

Ruined by one creep

The work of a team

Devoured by one tyrant

The spirit of life

Pounded down by the dead heads

The spirit of death

Exhumed by the living

The presence of dread

From a vampire of power

The start of a dream

Destroyed by one comment

The murder of swans

Not meant for the table

From the auto-destructive

Born of confusion

To the creation of hatred

Born of pure fact

Beaten and bloody

The spirit of sharing!

LADYBIRDS AND SPIDERS

Ladybirds and spiders
Who crawl across my wall
Their loveliness amazes me
And how they never fall

The architects of spiders' webs
All legs and pretty things
The beauty that embraces them
Their very special wings

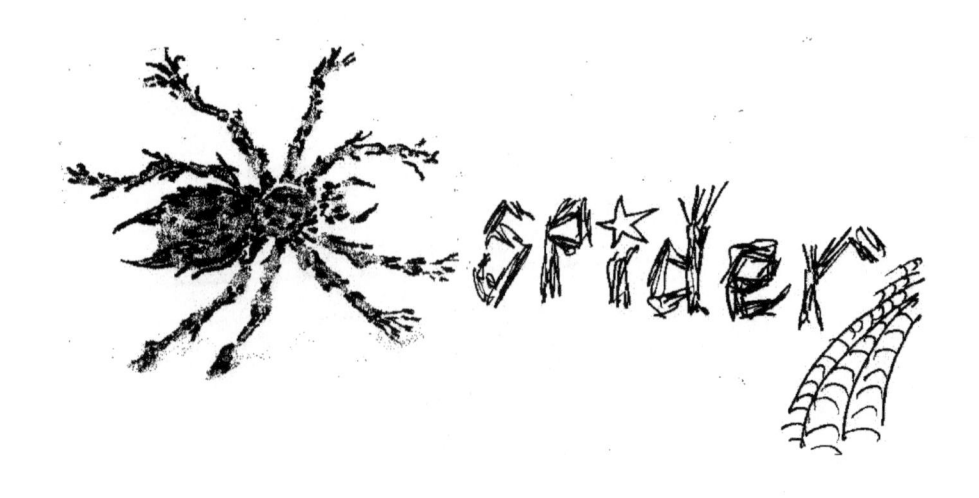

As they walk across my ceiling

With such graceful ease

Their very presence awe inspired

As if only there to please

If only I could speak with them

I'd like to tell them all

"Beware of horrid humans

Who'll try to squash you all."

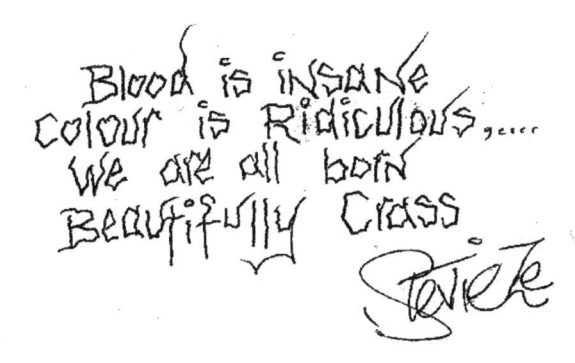

*Blood is insane
Colour is Ridiculous,....
We are all born
Beautifully Crass*

DAVID BOWIE AND MARC BOLAN

Working with David Bowie's 'Ziggy Stardust and the Spiders from Mars' lineup was such a thrill! Bass player Trevor Bolder produced and played on both my albums and I would often ask him questions about his Ziggy days. He once gave me a cd of Bowie in conversation about his close friendship with T Rex star Marc Bolan. How they met, and about their fashion tips for other artists who love to dress with originality and accordingly for the stage, as fashion statements are a mighty powerful and essential commodity for any artist who likes to project!

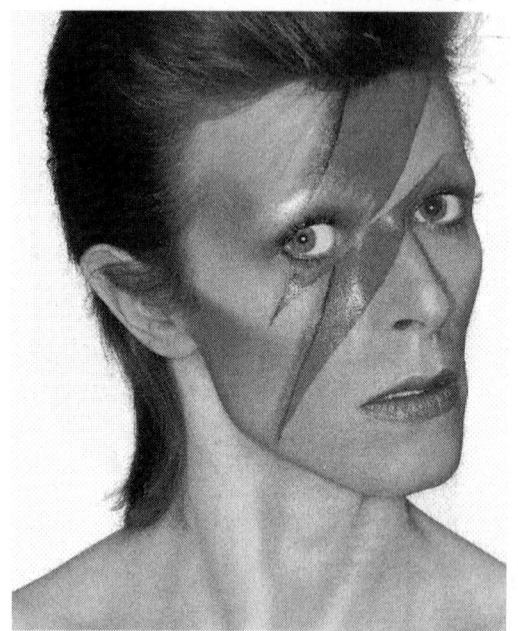

David spoke of how he and Marc Bolan would venture out at night to raid the bins down famous Carnaby Street, once the fashion capital of the world, along with Paris, during the sixties. Clothes designers such as Mary Quant would often discard unwanted remnants of their designer cuts, which would often end up outside in the bins. These remnants were still preciously useable for making jackets and shirts with that fabulous Carnaby Street look all of your own – and it worked!

All you needed was the right aptitude, and a needle and thread, and to know where to look. David and Marc would head out and have a good old rummage through it all for creative materials.

Bowie would exist on a diet of mainly milk and cuts of green or red peppers to keep his wafer-thin figure – and their early sixties wardrobe became second to none for imagination and originality.

Marc went for more outrageous silks, girls' shoes and satin jackets, whereas David teamed silks with baggy ladies style trousers, often with a long-sleeve blouse.

They remained close friends right up to Marc's untimely death in a fatal car crash in 1977. When David appeared as a special guest on what was to be Marc's last TV show, entitled 'Marc', they were having such fun, and it can clearly be seen that they were laughing so much that Marc fell off the stage at one point... almost like a warning of what was about to occur later that evening.

"I drive a Rolls Royce 'cos it's good for my voice."

Marc Bolan

Marc once said in an interview that he felt very strongly that he would not live long. He said he would probably die in a car crash like James Dean, who died in a Porsche... although he said he'd probably be in a mini or something... a weirdly accurate prediction as Marc sang in 'Jeepster'.

"Life is the same and it always will be

Easy as picking foxes from a tree"

Marc Bolan died at close to midnight on 16th September 1977 in a mini driven by his girlfriend Gloria Jones when they crashed into a tree in Barnes. The registration plate was FOX 661L.

He left this world a star.

Marc on stage at a sound check of The Damned

MY DEAD DAD

As winter falls
The bitter calls
In nightmares so immense
And so I wander all alone
'Til morning, so intense.

I have to see my father
He is shouting
Loud and dead
These images so meaningful
Still live inside my head
It's been so long
Yet no-one longs
For peace as much as I

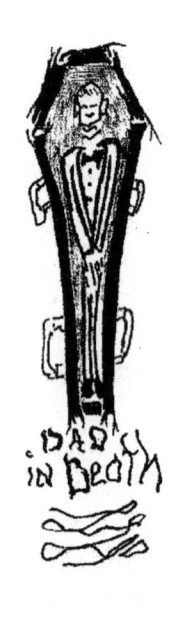

But in vain

The unexplained

Remains

As so will I

My body aches

With smell of oak

His coffin's white-wall tyres

Now rotting flesh

I must express

The peace my heart desires

ROCK & ROLL GUNSLINGERS

It isn't easy
watching heroes
as they fall

into the deepest
depths of Hell......
and as they haunt
the ancient corridors
of time, I
imagine stories
they could tell

this Beast of burden
is overgrown...
I pack my suitcase
and headed home!!!

for life's a prime evil
compromise
a crime you don't even
Realise.

LIVE AND LET DIE

The Inevitable Death Company Ltd

Do you worry about those final expenses when you die?

Well, with this wonderful life bringing you ever closer to that inevitable death of yours – we can help at Inevitable Death & Co Ltd.

Sign up with us for just a few pounds a week and we will take care of all those final, dismal details of yours. If you wish you may donate part, or all, of your house, your entire savings – which, let's face it, you will no longer need – your car, a computer, or anything else of great value.

We will gladly repay you with a loin cloth nightie to wear, fill up your veins with our total crap, and stick you in a cheap shitey little wooden box with your name engraved on the lid so we don't get you mixed up with the others. Your waterproof coffin is guaranteed for at least a year – even though you will be rotting away in it for an eternity. We've had no complaints about damp in our boxes so far!

When you sign with us you'll receive a cheap fountain pen to sign with, and a shitey little carriage clock so you can listen to the seconds tick away as you sit dribbling at the wall up to your final breath.

Contact Inevitable Death & Co Ltd today – before it's too late!

✝ the Reaper Waits

A symphony to the Devil
hope he likes our style...
inevitable...
I watch the maraudin' Lordies
as they Revel
in A symphony to the Devil

R.I.P

THE BIG 'MY WAY' SYNDROME

Fanfare to the common plank

And for all those dozy fuckers who request the song 'My Way' to be played at their funeral – when realistically, of course, you never did anything your way... did you?

In fact, you only ever did it 'the wife's way' or 'the boss's way' and took orders from shallow-minded, two-faced, social-climbing managerial Nazi scum! A jobsworth, a blundering, arse-wiping drip, paddling through what can only be described as a totally uneventful, dull existence.

Yes, a complete lifetime spent grovelling your way through, by doing only what you were told. And now, just because you are dead, you think you can suddenly come across as having been some kind of James Bond hero.

Well, sadly, you can't, cunt – as you are not now, and have never been an individual.

Fuck off... and good riddance!

R.I.P.

UK SUBS (PART 2)

GOURMET NIGHTS

During my long recovery from mental illness I found several outlets which bought me peace and contentment away from the torment and constant pressure of rock and roll.

One of these alternative passions was cooking – which I found extremely therapeutic and far from the world full of people I had just about given up on. No-one could antagonise or bully me in my kitchen – no matter how much mess I made!

By far the single most enjoyable breakfast I ever had was at the Thistle Hotel in Glasgow, where they served haggis at breakfast... Haggis for breakfast is something to die for. Please try it, there is also veggie haggis (?) and hash browns – it was absolutely wonderful.

In UK Subs I was the only one who didn't cook. The others were masters at it. There was Charlie with his wonderful roast dinners, and Alvin with his culinary skills, in particular his passion for Italian dishes and sauces – also his knowledge of Chinese fish dishes... sheer perfection! Nick, being a total vegetarian would come up with the tastiest gorgeous dishes I have ever had.

Whilst touring, we once used log cabins on a holiday camp in Holland as a base, out of season it was perfect. Each band member and crew had a chalet each and we had easy travel between shows in Europe.

Guitarist Nicky Garrett came up with 'Nick's Gourmet Night' on which we would all gather in his cabin after returning from a show to relax and eat great food. He cooked some of the most amazing dishes I have ever tasted in my life for both band and crew – he would cope very easily. Before a gig he'd pop into the local shops in Holland for supplies but would never tell us what the night's dish would be – and we always had a wonderful surprise.

The atmosphere was always so relaxed after a big show and I felt amongst friends and safe within my environment then. The band was so exciting and intense on stage and yet so close like a family really... but, back to Glasgow, where we played some of the most ferociously energetic gigs of our careers. Staying always at the Thistle Hotel and sampling the greatest hotel breakfast ever, of course. I always felt this strange energy and power about the place. I just loved it!

Plus in Scotland there was always a strange energy with the music because Scottish music is so alive and always has been. Then, across to Edinburgh, home of the great Fringe Festival with so many great artists and songwriters, and where you can always see my favourite jokesmith Tim Vine! Edinburgh is the arts, comedy, music and absolute food extravaganza for all the world to see.

WALES

In Wales we have always been made welcome and warm and whilst recording there at Rockfield Studio, in Monmouth, never would a weekend go by that we weren't asked if we needed any Sunday dinner, or anything. These things mean a lot when you're always away from home! One family I have always kept in touch with and will often visit whenever I'm there is Rob Kimber and his wife Carol, not forgetting their children Ronnie, Jade Peter and Liza.

So you see if you avoid the nasties, although there are many out there, you can build a whole brand new world around nice and caring people. This is what I have done and it works a treat!

Please don't ever feel lost or alone like I did as there is always lots of love and hope just around the corner.

Playing Cardiff Top Rank is a memory that will stay in my mind for ever. All my horrible enemies and critics were washed away in a second that night. You can all do the same, believe me.

I know that sanctuary is hard to find and memories can be so daunting but please try to go back to that special place or time of sheer happiness in your life, making you feel worthwhile again.

There have been such wonderful times but I will forever remember those UK Subs Gourmet Nights and Nick's magical kitchen. The best food, warmth, fun and friendship.

A true recipe for life.

SUN
As they played
purple haze
in a daze
from their Satellights
I'm just a beggar on the sand
take my hand
while I kiss the sky
and the troops,... in the fields
cannot feel,... so unreal
there's no reason why ?!??
All the futures in a child's
tiny hands,...
As it starts to cry

BE A RAINBOW

And they say

This is my space

And you're the wrong race

With the wrong hair

And you're far too poor

To be in my club

Not posh enough

To be in my pub

And this is my food

Although you are starving

You're not good enough

To be a council liar

Or an MP chancer

'Cos this is their world

And they own it all
They are the special breed
Who love a good free feed
On the common folk
Who are only good for votes

Forget the porridge oats
They want the caviar
And will destroy the world
As long as they are happy
And have lots of money

Like supermarket management
And desktop chancers
The property developer pinheads
And shirt and tie prancers

Whose shallow minds
You may depict
Yet hidden scum
You can't predict

Where beautiful punks
Are not allowed
My sweetly defiant
Belligerent crowd

Kill the animals too
They are just a nuisance
Scrub the pavements clean
And free of vermin
Like the poor and the homeless
In their cardboard boxes

And when they're all gone
Concrete the lot
Let the posh die alone
On their dull lifeless plots

For my beautiful punk will always be
The honest truth for all to see

Be a rainbow!

VISUAL IMAGERY

Visual imagery is vital.... people listen with their eyes !!

Stevie Z

"Get out of my life,
so I can
survive..."

"I'm a
human being"
StevieZe ©
from the album
"Auto Destructive"

"segregation + isolation
are peoples ignorance
toward difference"

StevieZe
Suicide

"If nobody hates you,....
your doing something wrong"
StevieZe

BOB DYLAN

Bob Dylan was the man who spoke the truth. A songwriting genius who didn't care a shit about what other people might think of him.

When I was at my all-time lows I would switch on to his realities on life and people's torment.

This created a calm within my soul – a peace that knowing someone else possessed the same feelings as I did about the unjustness and unfairness of human beings. The greed, hunger and cruelty of a planet full of people who don't give a shit about anyone but themselves.

What do you see, my blue-eyed son

What do you feel, my darling young one?

Bob Dylan

Bob Dylan – you always only spoke the truth.

THE STORYTELLER

the Storyteller

Bishops + swords
conflict + wars
castles + kings
Angels with wings

Warriors of defience
Vampires + Giants
Spacemen of silence
Witches galore

Princess in Lace
dancers with Grace
Kings of abduction
Queens of seduction

planets + Meteors
Earths finest creatures
Ivory towers
Preachers + teachers

Alien Beings
Steeples of empathy
energy vampires
Maidens of sympathy

dogsflesh + termites
vice + starlights
Gravestones in headlights
Sensational twilights

2ND CLASS CITIZEN

No time

For compromise

Between the elitist greed

And political liars

No rights

No freedom of speech

You're a second class citizen

On you own streets

We need a Wild Riot Revolution

Before the end of evolution

We need a Wild Riot Revolution

For all time

A revolution, baby

An evolution

You're a second class citizen

Without a revolution, baby

No peace

Just tax police

No human rights

No freedom to speak

No air to breathe

No books to read

Just the energy vampires

With a need to feed

We need a Wild Riot Revolution

Before the end of evolution

We need a Wild Riot Revolution

That's no crime

IT'S ONLY RAIN

Cloudy skies are raining down

On me... tonight

How I needed something I believe

Is right

And I needed you

Just to help me through

Cloud hides the sun up in the sky so bright

Looks like it's raining down on me... for life

And I've needed you, do you need me too?

Don't stop the rain from coming down

It's all I ever have, and ever wanted

Now it's all around, yet cloudy skies

Can never cause me pain

It's only rain

HANOI ROCKS

Drummer Razzle – one of the good guys

While UK Subs was touring quite intensely in and around Finland we came across a fabulous rock band. They would turn up in an old school bus in which they all lived, complete with girlfriends, PA, lighting rig and backline.

We didn't realise how great they were until they opened for us in Copenhagen one wintery, snow-filled evening. As they took to the stage they looked a million dollars! Highly charismatic vocalist Mike Monroe, who also played a mean saxophone with such class. We knew immediately that these guys were potential stars and must be helped over to Britain and possibly on to better things.

The name of this great band – HANOI ROCKS.

We continued our tour and asked them to join us for the duration – and to our delight they agreed. They opened for us each night in such a star-spangled way that by the time the tour finished we had become very good friends.

We suggested that they should come back to England with us, as we knew several management companies who would just love to take them on… they agreed and over they came, lock stock and barrel – with one exception. Mike Monroe, Andy McCoy, Sam Yaffa and Nasty Suicide came over but their drummer decided to stay in Finland as he had a new young family.

On arrival in the UK we introduced them to manager Richard Bishop who was determined to find the next Rolling Stones! And remember, this is all pre- Guns and Roses. Richard took them on and soon signed them to a major label for release in the States. The year is 1980, and the scene is now set. However – they needed a drummer.

Now, there was a pub off Fleet Street, London, where everyone in bands used to hang out for some of the most outrageous liquid lunches ever to take place between tours. And, in those days, music press such as Melody Maker, NME and Sounds, all had offices nearby. I forget the pub's name, but frequent visitors to this establishment were a band called The Wall – who had a great drummer known to all as Razzle.

He was a lovely guy who carried an image totally befitting to Hanoi Rocks from Finland. Razz always wore a top hat, and used eye-liner, so when Hanoi Rocks walked in, as pre-arranged by us and Melody Maker editor Carol Clark, it was obvious to everyone he was born to be in this band. I introduced him and he joined the band immediately!

Razzle settled in straight away and Hanoi Rocks was soon heading for America, where they went down an absolute storm, influencing many big bands like Guns and Roses. Sadly though tragedy was about to strike all too soon and it would be devastating.

They were all at a rock and roll barbeque held by the outrageous band Motley Crew on Huntingdon Beach, California on December 8th 1984. Sex, drugs and much hard partying was in full flow with everyone having a ball when Motley Crue singer Vince Neil decided he needed to go out to top up supplies.

Fatefully he took Razzle with him and they set off at high speed in Neil's 1972 De Tomaso Pantera. They arrived at a notoriously dangerous crossroads at well over the speed limit. The resulting violent collision was so devastating that Neil's Pantera was left as an unrecognisable wreck. Razzle was pronounced dead at the scene – amazingly Neil survived!

It was reported that the ferocity of the impact ripped off one of Razzle's cowboy boots and it was left standing in the middle of the road, with the mangled car steaming in the background.

Ironically the party continued through the night, although many disappeared after hearing the news which turned it into a sombre affair, with everyone in shock and sadness.

To the best of my knowledge a picture of Razzle still hangs on a wall of the pub where it all began.

Goodnight my lovely friend.

HANOI ROCKS

Razzle (Nicholas Dingley) 1960 – 1984

Much potential but plagued with heartbreak.

I AM A PLANT

My God
I am a plant...
I'd love to dance
but can't...
However I can grow
& make my colours
glow...
I'll help you
when your sad...
give joy when you feel bad,

congradulate your high's
or help you re-arise
give comfort if you cry
& bless you when you die.....

thats why I am a plant
making sure your all enhanced
inriched in visual spirits bloom
bringing endless sunshine
HOME TO YOU !!
cc

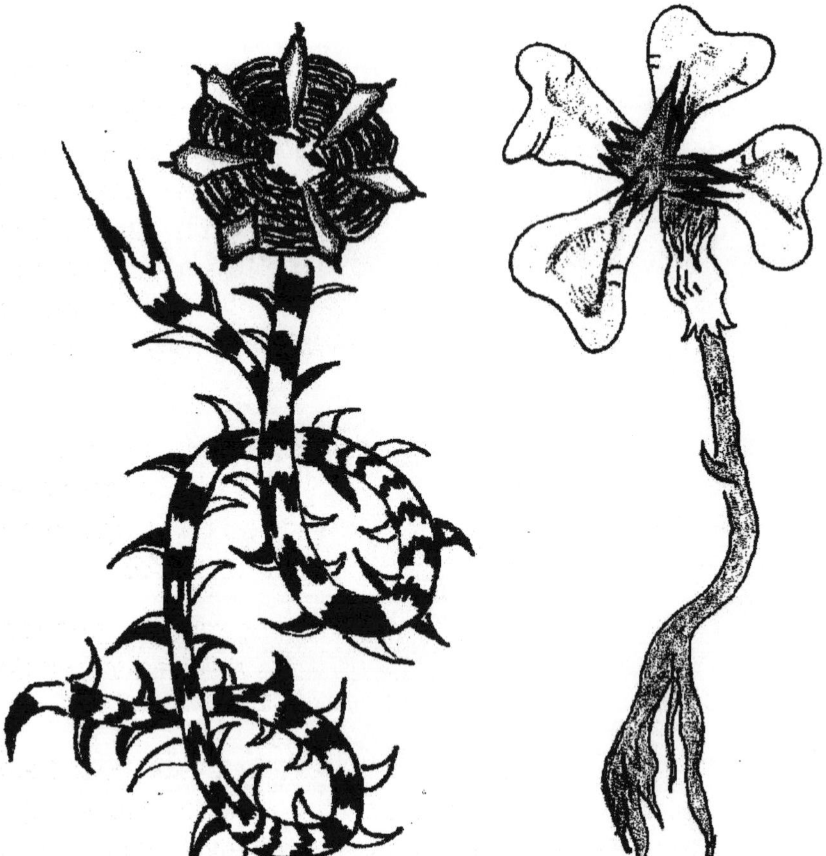

THE RAMONES

As I entered the dimly lit, silently superb atmospheric bar and walked towards the stage a shiver of sheer excitement ran through me. Here I was finally in New York City, home of such musical history involving punk in particular… for this was not just another punk venue nor an extra sell out date on our UK Subs tour of America – this was the legendary CBGB's, where some of the most influential bands started off. This was the true home of the American punk scene, filled with the ghosts of sheer genius which were born here.

From New York Dolls to Blondie and Talking Heads, plus the godfather himself, Iggy Pop, who gave some of the most exciting performances of his entire career right here on this stage! Now I was about to play that very stage with my band UK Subs.

What a huge thrill! The graffiti in the dressing rooms alone read like a who's who history lesson, as the walls seemed to just drip nostalgia.

As I sat at the bar before the show, watching our gear being loaded in, I wondered who had sat there before me – Jayne County and the Electric Chairs, maybe the Velvet Underground, maybe even the B52's, possibly even my all-time favourites, the Psychedelic Furs – 'Pretty in Pink!'

But all this paled into insignificance against the musical birthplace of Johnny, Dee Dee, Marky and Joey – of course I'm talking about the mighty Ramones! The most powerfully driving band I have ever seen in my entire life – for UK Subs had already completed a highly successful world tour with the Ramones – a historical event indeed, and something to be proud of.

Our tour manager, Stephen 'Chutch' Drury, was a total star, organising and taking on the responsibility for everyone with his absolute professional perfection!

So, for the sake of our young people of today, let me explain to you just what the Ramones were – for now seeing the name once again on fashionable tops and T shirts being worn by young people, 90% of whom probably don't even know what that word means. Well. I'll tell you.

The Ramones were the greatest, loudest, most exciting band ever. Please check out their live double album called 'It's Alive'. They would start their show with singer Joey announcing "Hi, we're the Ramones, and this one's called… "then bass player Dee Dee would shout the count in "One, Two, Three, Four," and they were off!

The Ramones at CBGB's

Each song was a pure statement and played as loud as loud can be, as loud as Hell, in fact, right through to the end of the show, by which time your body felt physically traumatised, with ears ringing in the aftermath of being in the presence of Rock and Roll legends.

As each song finished, Dee Dee would be shouting the four beat count in then they were straight into the next song. There were no breaks between the songs, no hesitation, thus creating total rock and roll mayhem from start to finish – and I loved it! I loved their shows, I loved their loudness, and I loved their image projection. Each sporting leather jackets, jeans ripped at the knees, and white plimmies and T shirts.

And Chutch held that tour together somehow – in his usual superb, dependable and professional way. When I said to Chutch afterward, "Thanks, and well done, matey," he simply replied, "No probs, I learned from the best – Dave 'Dad' Leaper." I smiled and we all agreed.

That night we played like obsessed demons, as if their very spirit had entered our bodies. The place was alive with noise, sweat and mayhem – and surrounded of course with beautiful historic chaos.

So the mighty Ramones may have left us now for ever, yet their musical legacy will remain intact always as the driving force they were in rock and roll history.

Guitarist Johnny Ramone once said,

> "Learn to stand with your guitar looking great
>
> Then, and only then, learn to play it!"

ENTER THE BEATLES

"My guitar is now an audible weapon for what's inside."

Stevie Ze

All these things can destroy your confidence and bring you crashing down. My most major breakdown occurred when my doggie Cassie died. At that time I had already lost my father and brother, yet it was Cassie who finally finished me off, as I was so totally shattered at losing her.

Several situations can lead to breakdown... money, bereavement as in the loss of a loved one, or in my case a pet. It could also, of course, be career loss. All are a common cause of depression and anxiety which can stop you in your tracks without help.

For years I have been in a kind of mourning for my beloved bands, in particular UK Subs, for being in a line-up like that – and I mean me with Charlie, Nick and Alvin, which was a dream come true, and without them I felt both lost and useless.

Going from Top of the Pops to mopping floors in a fish and chip shop every morning is a long way to fall, believe me! Yet this was to the cruel delight of many local musicians. Now to be hailed as a loser, a freeloader, a waste of space, while unable to pick myself up through lack of money was devastating.

Suddenly you are trapped inside a deep hole which sent me on a deep spiral of depression and alcohol abuse which I could not control. The worst comments were in the form of "Ha ha, look at the big rock star now!" and "There's a guy works down the chip shop thinks he's Elvis."

I lost my entire family forever while I was suffering in this condition – and all of this from those who just don't realise the tremendous hurt, pain and mental strain that they are causing.

On the other hand there are those who really love what you've done and are so complimentary and wish to shake your hand, plus, of course, the obligatory selfie which I will always gladly go along with as it's my absolute pleasure to give. Make someone smile every day and you are a star – but it a very cruel existence when you no longer feel worthy of the adulation any more.

So – a bunch of people love you, another bunch hate the sight of you, and the rest are left wondering who the hell you are, constantly staring dumb-faced at you, blank and bewildered.

Many deaths and other upsets will inevitably occur during someone's lifetime, be it in the workplace, on the sports pitch, losing someone you love through divorce or breakup, or simply by being dumped. Since no longer being in a well-known band I have now been dumped by so many who I had always thought were true friends – I can hardly describe just how painful this is.

A lack of understanding towards mental health issues does not help either. Becoming labelled 'different' or 'freaky' by the media, or hearing the terms 'bent' or 'queer' also applied is so ignorantly abusive and offensive.

One of the great bands who have helped me through this with their lyrics is The Kinks – and the words of Ray and Dave Davis. 'Death of a

Clown is a wonderfully poignant piece of work, then there's the frighteningly truthful 'Sunny Afternoon'. So if you can find comfort in song lyrics, take a listen to the Kinks. I suggest you also try other writers including James Taylor's 'You got a Friend,' and 'Fire and Rain,' also the epic 'Sweet Baby James,' then there are the wonderfully moving lyrics of Cat Stevens, now known as Usef Islam, with 'Moon Shadow,' or 'Morning has Broken'.

You can see here the differentiation between angst and anger, and the need to feel a comfort blanket through a beautiful melody. When I feel anger or frustration, especially towards the negative feelings of the masses, I'll turn to the Rolling Stones' 'Honky Tonk Women.' That track has such a great groove by drummer Charlie Watts. Or 'Get off my Cloud,' which still fills me with energy and an injection of adrenalin just like it did when I was seventeen years old!

Going deeper I have Marilyn Manson or Slipknot to explore, and in sad reflective mode there is the touching 'Love of my Life' or UK Subs' 'Sensitive Boys' from the Diminished Responsibility album. Then even Mozart, and 'The Planets' by Gustav Holst!

Enter the Beatles

Eventually I get to The Beatles – where all this love of music started. It began with a vinyl LP – or album – which my grandad purchased for me from a second-hand shop in Bury, Lancashire... a gift I still treasure to this day. And the name of this mind-awakening album? A Hard Day's Night by The Beatles.

Now when I pick up my guitar it's like an audible weapon. So no-one can stop me or put me down any more, and my music is fuelled by sheer angst, determination and a new love of life. Even my soft ballads and pop songs are all a huge barrier I have erected to keep out the horrendous so-called friends of the past, and to stop them from upsetting me any more after they all disappeared.

I am now a songwriter, poet, musician, author and performer – and so happy in my own space, and these are the things they can no longer take off me... ever!

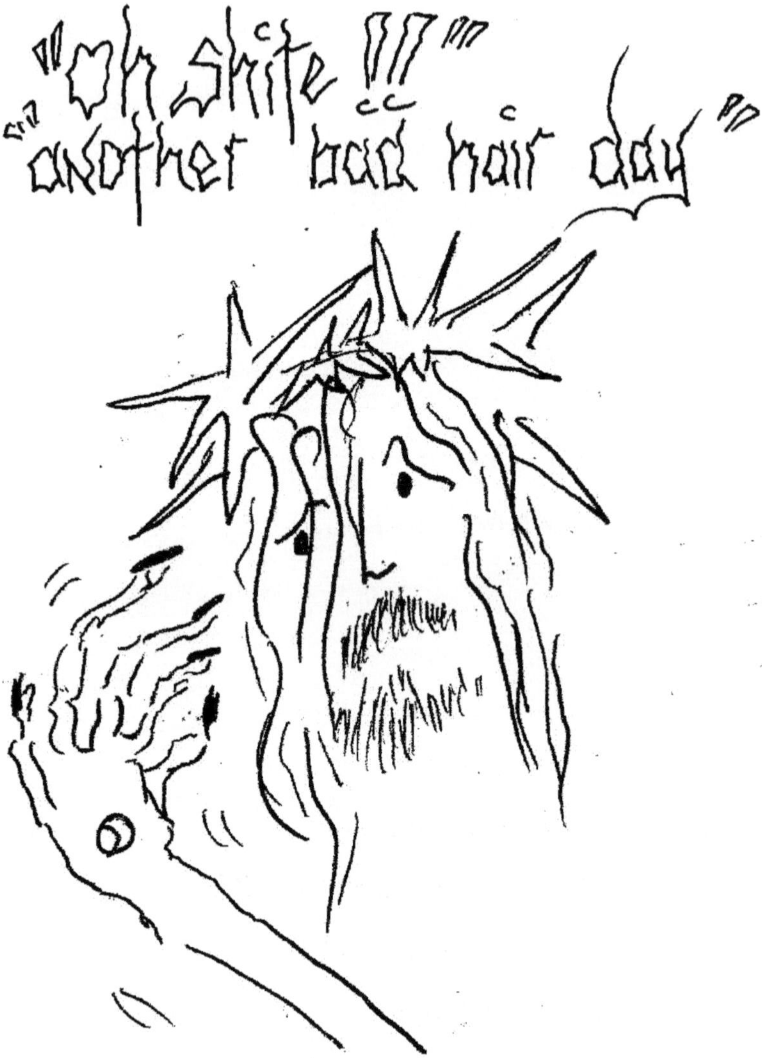
"oh shite !!"
"another bad hair day"

INTO THE VOID

Into the void, into the void

We are cross collateralisation

A must to avoid

In the circus of needless

We are making some NOIZE

So get out of the darkness

Ignition deployed

Into the void, into the void

We are dematerialisation

Existence devoid

In a circus of anticipation

We are making some NOIZE

So out of the darkness

Ignition deployed

Into the void, the rain goes on

As the eye can see

Dripping shades of pure empathy

The circus is closed now

We are making some NOIZE

So, at this point of darkness

Ignition deployed

HellRAiza

I stand and stare
into the grave,
of Mankinds
egotistic ways,
black roses
cover everywere,
a dark pollution
fills the air,...

And nothing's
ever gonna change,
these psychic Night-
-Mares fill with rain

My death

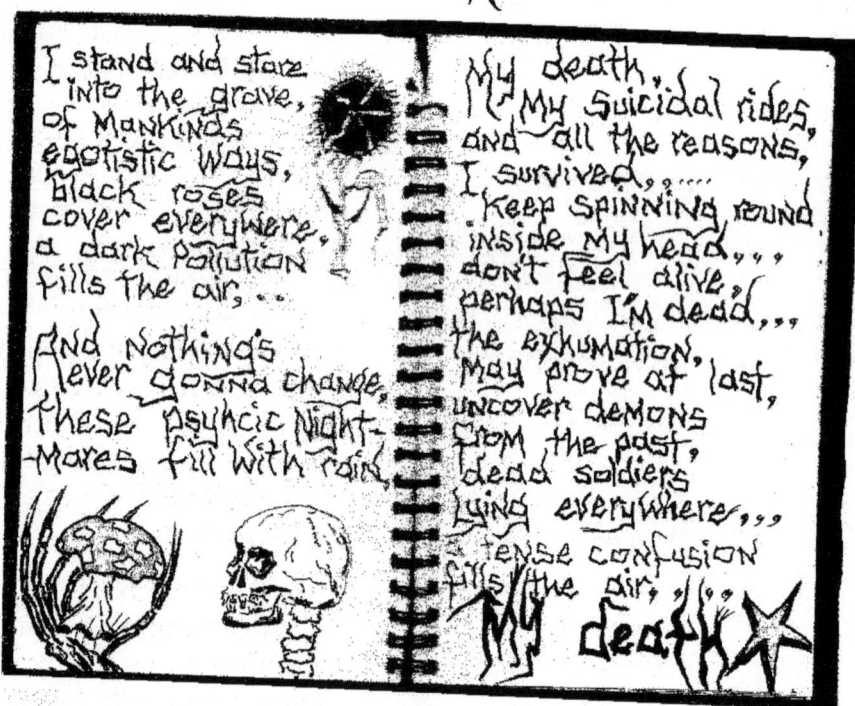

My death,
My suicidal rides,
and all the reasons,
I survived,,....
keep spinning round
inside my head,,,,
don't feel alive,
perhaps I'm dead,,,
the exhumation,
may prove at last,
uncover demons
from the past,
dead soldiers
lying everywhere,,,
tense confusion
fills the air,,,,,,
My death

UK SUBS (PART 3)

New sleeve notes from Diminished Responsibility

Re-released by Demon Records November 2019

Steve Roberts aka Stevie ZeSuicide

The first album I recorded with UK Subs was Diminished Responsibility – just prior to a sold-out 63 date British tour. We opened at Cardiff Top Rank – a huge venue packed to the rafters. Down in the dressing room we could hear the chant "UK Subs!" "UK Subs!" over and over, accompanied by the stomping of a couple of thousand Doc Martens. It was like thunder – a little frightening but wonderful. The fans went wild as we appeared and went into C.I.D. and I want to thank all the kids there for making it so very special.

We had finished recording the new album, but at that time, didn't have a title for it. Following Charlie's great alphabetical plan it had to start with the letter D. In the hotel lift with Nick he was telling me about some rock and roll high jinks like throwing TV's out of windows and trashing rooms that had gone on – maybe with AC/DC and crew who were in the same hotel – but I said I would claim diminished responsibility if accused. Nick said, "That's IT! That's the new title." Later Charlie and Alvin agreed.

These days were a dream come true. Charlie: the ultimate frontman, genius songwriter, performer, and personality. Nick: the most exciting and dangerous presence on stage bar none. Alvin: the complete rock/punk star in his own right with his low-slung bass and devilish moves.

Often imitated but never outclassed – UK Subs were simply the best. More stories can be found in Rock & Roll Chronicles, written as Stevie ZeSuicide and available on Amazon.

Originally released in early 1981 "Diminished Responsibility" was the U.K. Subs fourth album and it reached NO.18 in the British National Chart.

Release information

Label: Demon Records • Format: Vinyl • Date: 29/11/2019

Cat#: UKSUBSDEM004 • Barcode: 5014797899643

Genre: Rock Sub Genre: Punk

STEPHEN 'CHUTCH' DRURY

Stephen James Drury, fondly known as 'Chutch', was our tour manager and top man with UK Subs for many of our world tours of 'chaotic jet set vandalism.'

He was also with Cyanide on tour, and, of course, the mighty Ramones at the height of punk rock. Together with top sound man Dave Leaper, you couldn't have wished for a better crew!

We would have a great time on the road playing to packed houses with the most loyal fans you could dream of.

Chutch was the first one in York to discover punk rock power – and he also got me into Ziggy Stardust, Lou Reed and Black Sabbath.

He is now an extremely talented, award-winning photographer, Pictured here with me at the old Music Machine bar. Great days – truly a lifetime well spent! I am proud to know him.

'Chutch' - a lifetime of creativity!

ENTER THE WHO

Mary Quant miniskirts, The Kinks and Mini Coopers

My obsession with music and art had reached an all-time high during my secondary school years, aged twelve and thirteen. Carnaby Street fashion and The Small Faces had by now introduced me to a wonderful new world of Mary Quant dresses and skirts, Biba hipsters, Mini Coopers and long, long hair!

However I was to struggle for my passions and battle the elements of opposition, both from my father - a jazz musician all the way – and school teachers with uncontrollable perilous self-superiority, consumed by non-thought and total fashion ignorance and discrimination. Things were different in those days, where lack of understanding and tolerance or forethought were within our education system!

At school I was being pushed into nowhere land without any choice – and I hated it! So, arriving at yet another crossroad, one more major change in my life was about to occur. When I saw The Kinks and The Who, both live on TV it was awesome, but the best was yet to come. Trapped now by school and all its rubbish nonsense I was confused and in need of direction.

But then, hang fire, for sure enough, one day a heavy hand landed on my shoulder. "The headmaster wants to see you now!" I was ordered by a servant cretin of the Almighty Big One!

I had already started experimenting with wearing eye liner, yet didn't think anyone seemed to notice until now. So at first I assumed that this was the reason for such a strong summons – as even the girls at school weren't allowed to wear makeup.

This headmaster had always appeared quite nice up to this point. He seemed to be a gentle giant of a man, as opposed to my past headmaster who totally ignored you as riff raff – plus looked like a retarded midget with a huge oversized head like an ugly deranged carnival doll. This one, however, had massive oversized feet in shitty brown shoes, and always with Scottish tartan socks. How bizarre that when you are twelve everyone over twenty is a weirdo!

As I waited outside his office the clock on the wall ticked like a death watch beetle. By now my knees were trembling in fear of what I had done wrong. Eventually I was called in and stood silently before his large desk.

I stood alone.

On the wall were two famous portraits, 'When did you last see your father?' by William Frederick, and the fabulous 'Blue Boy' by Thomas Gainsborough – both set in beautiful gilded frames.

An old grandfather clock ticked even louder as the Head didn't even look up at me. Was I a mere fly waiting to be swatted? Or a young person, victim of silent endless bullying from a nobody?

Finally I was granted an audience as he looked up, twirled his pencil and just glared at me. I was terrified at this point and he knew it! I knew he couldn't actually murder me, as that was against the law, however there are some things in life which are far worse than death, but I wasn't quite sure at this point exactly what they were.

He tapped his nails erratically on his desk in obvious frustration at my very presence. I shuddered to think what he could possibly accuse me of that was so vile as to warrant such drama-packed angst. There was a glaring silence which seemed to last forever, then his big gob finally opened. "Well, boy!" he bellowed, "We have a problem, don't we?" I quaveringly replied, "I don't know, sir," in what was the smallest voice ever heard in the history of mankind to this day.

"Is there something wrong with you, boy?"

"No, sir," I replied.

"Well, it has been bought to my attention that you have chosen needlework as a subject."

"Yes, sir."

"I suggest you give this much thought, my lad," he snapped, "And strongly consider changing your mind to woodwork or metalwork like the rest of the boys in this school." My silence was answered with, "I presume you are a boy?"

I replied angrily and flippantly, "Well I must be a girl then, sir." This only infuriated the 'Big Sir' even further, especially when I added, "And I don't play rugby either."

And so I was ordered to amend my gender blip with immediate effect and placed in metalwork. Now, having been robbed of my Mary Quant fashion designer dream I felt so lost, as becoming an artist had also slipped away from me having been referred to as "an insult to a pencil" by my then art teacher Mr (Small Head) Longdon, another prick who I'd looked up to at one point!

All that was left for me now was music and rock and roll, in fact. Turning totally to my drums, and as an admirer of Keith Moon in particular, creating extremely loud chaos, anarchy and destruction. The destruction of all this boredom.

From now on the only true idols were up on that stage!

My dad's drummer from Caesar's Palace called me "Hopelessly duff, and way too loud a player for anything." This from a person who I had always idolised and admired during my school days. He once came to my school and I was so proud – this made his comments hurt even more. But it was all 'big-time' nonsense, he clearly thought nothing of me as an artist or drummer. I was just as duff as everyone else in his eyes. Except I wasn't exactly duff, dickhead, was I?

I had met the greatest drummer in the world, Buddy Rich, and he was really nice and encouraging to me, which was just what I needed at the time. I had a picture with him, and his autograph, which was so precious to me – yet it was stolen from me by a spoilt, "I want" mummy's boy at school to whom it meant nothing.

It seemed that life was becoming put down after put down until I'd just about had enough of it all.

ENTER THE WHO

Then The Who's Pete Townshend walked on stage during Woodstock Festival in 1969 and announced "This is where it all ends!" before launching into 'My Generation.' It was the peace and love bit as well, so after The Mama's and Papa's, Joni Mitchell, Canned Heat, Peter Paul and Mary, Crosby Still and Nash, and The Moody Blues, it was just right for some rebellion – and at last here it was!

Apparently backstage before the Woodstock show Pete had been in quite a bitter argument with Jimi Hendrix over the running order. Jimi had said he was not going on after The Who, to which Pete replied "Well, we're definitely NOT going to follow you on!"

This argument continued back and forth until Pete finally finished it with "Look, final word, we are NOT going on after you – and don't forget, it's OUR gear on stage!" At this, Jimi knew he had to back down but he simply stood up on a chair and performed the most amazing guitar ever seen! He stated that if he had to go on after The Who he was going to pull out all the stops. And he did, famously setting fire to his guitar then smashing it to pieces during the song 'Wild Thing.' A memorable performance indeed after a superb set by him and a major piece of rock and roll history was created!

Then… the ultimate masterpiece – a masterclass in rock and roll and how it should be done.

'We Won't get Fooled Again' was released by The Who. This symbolised life to me and after 'My Generation' previously I had my education on a plate.

What followed was a succession of fabulous music and styles to lift my spirits and keep me going.

The Stones' 'Honky Tonk Women' and 'Jumping Jack Flash', The Kinks' 'Waterloo Sunset', 'Dead End Street', 'Follower of Fashion', Peter Sarsted's 'Where do You go to my Lovely?' to name but a few – and you can add to this London and Paris fashions, Carnaby Street, and Mini Coopers.

Playing in bands I became loud, obnoxious, and rebellious inside, which I quickly found in The Rolling Stones, Bob Dylan, and above all, the mighty Jimi Hendrix – all leading me up to my eventual glam rock splendour! A dedicated follower of fashion, if you like!

I now made sure that the big head bull shite brigade could no longer dare to come anywhere near me! I was free!

"And when he pulls his frilly nylon panties right up tight

He feels a dedicated follower of fashion."

Ray Davis

MAD ALBERT

Mad Albert was a well-known figure in York City Centre as he roamed the streets, shouting at everyone to "Get lost!" or, his favourite expression, to "Buck off!" – though strangely, and for reasons unexplained, he would never use the F word itself! Yet he would quite happily shout at the tourists and traffic 'til he reached home – much to everyone's relief! In fact the police got so used to his bizarre antics that when it got bad they would simply drive him out into the countryside then drop him off to walk all the way home in peace!

Despite his language Albert was never offensive, in fact after shouting in your face he would smile at you with his wonderful toothless grin. It was a smile that would warm your heart – after you'd been told to "Buck off!" that is! "Can you move it?" was another of his expressions, or "Go on, move it!" Mad Albert is now a legend in the city of York and, just like Dick Turpin, he certainly did exist.

When punk started all the local punks loved and adored this eccentric old man in the flat cap and raincoat. He meant to harm to anyone and everyone knew it. Here he is, pictured with myself, Bob DeFries and 'Dave Zef' Stewart when we were Cyanide.

I always wondered if he was mad – or was it the rest of the world?

50 SHADES OF DEATH (PT 1)

Come with me, I'll show you something
Of hatred seeped in mass oppression
The boss is nothing, his wife is no-one
Their stinking lives are climbing vermin
So go to Hell or stop complaining
Or disappear without explaining
And, like their wives who clearly don't care
With such blatant greed they so feed my anger
It's oil or gold - their monotonous babble
Like desperate beggars, in arts they dabble
When all this time we dance and tango
Whilst others starve in life's fandango
A well-washed monarch is nothing better
In earlier times they'd have your head off!
As cheats desire be-suited triers
How cash inspires their crass built empires
Property pigs of sheer embezzlement
Overcharge students extortionate closet rent

Yet remain content about the rules they've bent

Then students grow to deliver no hope

Become politicians for what it's worth

Talking old rope, dopes grabbing votes

Cut their hair just like Blair

Send us stupids off to a war

While they stay at home earning more and more

Our MP's practice total hate

All you need is a good liar's face

With cadaver dead eyes and a stupid grin

Like a comsat angel laced with gin

If this is life then I don't want it

If quality's what's inside your wallet

Then let me live alone in peace

Away from it all, the human race

Don't be obscene like all the rest

Whose concrete lives are not the best

Peace of mind for what it's worth

Is looking up to life on Earth

"Kindness is the new rebellion"

Pink

50 SHADES OF DEATH (PT 2)

From church admirers' dark desires

To skinless priests destroyed by fire

Bones of rust consumed by dust

Tell ancient tales of endless lust

Self-righteous fools and bleating weasels

Paint their rules upon burning easels

Stinking zombies rattle around

As they turn to mould beneath the ground

Big head, dead head, naked preachers

Dig new graves, the vilest creatures

Naked vampires wait to devour

After Holy wars with nuclear power

Headless butchers of wretched torment

Throw ragged dolls in pittance thrust

From Hounds of Hell black spit expires

In relentless, plague-ridden vomit-soaked attire

Arriving late, and in denial

With rancid seeds to which impale

More victims scream at Vlad's command

Forgiveness day is close at hand

The 'O' in God is not so hollow

As acid rains in the trough of sorrow

Denying monks of sex decline

Prepare their sermons trapped in time

Monks may die, the traitors cry

But revenge is sweet, like apple pie

It's not a lot to share your bread

While hate-filled spitefuls seethe with dread

But know-alls and big heads and upright dead

Are just maggot-infested walking death!

"You sound like a hillbilly – we need folk singers here!"
Quote from a 60's New York coffee bar owner to Bob Dylan

CANNED HEAT

Together we stand – Divided we fall

Come on now people – Let's get on the ball

And work together –come on come on – let's work together

Make someone happy – Make someone smile

Come on now people – Let's make life worthwhile

And work together –come on come on – let's work together

Come on you people – Walk hand in hand

Let's make this world of ours – A good place to stand

Because together we will stand

Every boy, girl, woman and man…

Lyrics and music © Harrison 'Bob the Bear' Hite and
Alan 'Blind Owl' Wilson

WITCHFINDER GENERALS

...Still EXIST - shocker!!!

Witchfinders (modern day, shallow, cruel, bastard, interfering, busybody shite-stirrers) can all still be found in various befitting employment situations: supermarket managers, police, traffic wardens, parish councillors, local churches, resident associations, the Rotary Club, golfers, BMW drivers, priests, monks, security guards, teachers, town councils, magistrates, judges!

All must be avoided – at all costs – in order to prevent your bringing down, or even mental ruination, because all of these of which I speak are totally brain dead...

The brain dead big head

Know-all maggot-infested

Walking death

Stevie Ze

(from 50 Shades of Death)

LOU REED – TRANSFORMER

By now, out of much darkness Lou Reed's fabulous album 'Transformer' came back into my life. I now had my own little world – Planet Stevie – if you like, in which I felt safe and wanted again.

My music became a major turning point and Stevie ZeSuicide was born out of this sheer anxiety and love of sound! I took the name from David Bowie's 'Rock and Roll Suicide' and now wore my guitar like a protective machine gun, totally devoid of fear or any outsiders' negative influences. Where bad can no longer penetrate, no-one can take it away, come near it, or stop me, anymore!

To create music or anything

Without interference from outsiders

Is to create reality

Stevie Ze

A SOLDIER'S STORY

WO2 James 'Harry' Roberts

My brother was blown up twice in Afghanistan whilst attempting, along with his colleagues, to restore both peace and harmony, but most importantly, freedom for all.

Freedom so that teenagers can be teenagers and women can receive some respect for a change – and young ladies can enjoy life and be allowed to grow up having fun! Allowed to own a mobile phone of their own , a TV in their room allowing them to watch what they want – in short the basic little luxuries which every child deserves to possess as part of them finding themselves in life. Something they haven't been allowed to do!

A computer link to the outside world, plus boyfriends or girlfriends of their own choice, seriously enjoying modern fashions and young people's music just like anyone else in this modern world.

Growing up normally without persecution from the bullying paranoid Noddy boys in white dresses who wish to keep them imprisoned and out of sight – while they grow their beards and big 'moustaches, no doubt to look like their old mothers, who we also never see.

I am so sick inside, and so tired of witnessing Eastern streets filled with hairy-faced angry men screaming their hatred of everything whilst burning Western flags – with no sight of a female anywhere!

My brother retired from active duty after suffering from extremely serious internal injuries. He had also served in Northern Ireland and Iraq for everything he thought was right. On his return to civvy street his own private battle began in his head. The nightmare horrors, deaths and hatred he had witnessed and endured are beyond comprehension to the everyday person. This all eventually took its toll on him and he left us all totally devastated.

He would often say, "Why did my friends die? Why not me?" He never spoke about it much but on one occasion he had to bag up pieces of his commanding officer after their vehicle was destroyed by a land mine. James had been sitting next to the officer who was killed instantly in the explosion – and this was shortly after they had been sitting having breakfast together with no idea of what the short future held.

Together we stand – divided we fall

Come on now people – let's get on the ball

And work together

Because together we will stand

Every boy, girl, woman and man

Canned Heat

I believe that young people should be free to grow up with respect and equality for all, especially towards women and young girls, and not to be taught prejudice, or have to witness inhibitions from the so-called 'grown-ups' of doom and gloom.

Teach them peace and understanding – but most importantly let them be free to live a normal life of their own choosing.

Our Jamie died on 7th November 2010. After his death I felt extremely distressed, and filled with a totally frustrating anger. My drinking vastly increased as I was now filled with a hate and resentment and started to despise everything all around me – everything!

Now consumed by a passion for revenge in whatever form for these atrocities. I became isolated and extremely unsociable – often getting into trouble with the law over cheap comments constantly fired at me over my appearance. I should have been used to it yet it started to hit home very hard indeed. I didn't like this in myself and decided to take drastic action to try to eradicate these thoughts. I asked a Muslim friend of mine to take me to his mosque. I just had to find out for myself once and for all. He agreed and off we went!

I have to admit I was quite nervous and apprehensive about how I would be received with my pink hair, earrings, nail polish – the whole look! I felt I had to do this, though, for my own peace of mind, or live in eternal torment towards something about which I had no accurate information whatsoever. Would I survive? Would I be thrown off a high building to my death? Or what? What did happen had me pleasantly astonished. I was welcomed with open arms and total friendship and support, offered food and good conversation on all sorts of topics – including the wrongs of terror! I walked away from there afterwards feeling a much better person for merely going in and finding out for myself. I'm so glad I did it.

I have visited many places of worship during my travels abroad – and it was in Singapore I was to find out and witness the wondrously diverse cultures which our beautiful world has to offer us. I'm talking about temples of splendour, all accompanied by the most fabulous food dishes – Hindu, Sikh, Muslim, and more – and although I have never taken on board any religion of my own these wonders of beauty that surround us all are to be cherished, embraced and loved. We are all so special – if only we knew! None of these who have given service and sacrificed their lives during all the wars in history, in order to create a modern world of freedom and democracy should ever be forgotten, or taken for granted. After all they did it for us who survive. Their fear, pain, suffering, home sickness, shell shock, sadness, loss, and eventual death was endured to for our future freedom.

We must never forget them all – EVER!

"I care about decency and humanity and kindness. Kindness today is the new rebellion. There are people who don't have what we have – help them get it. It feels good to help. It feels powerful to help. Stop fighting each other and help each other."

Pink

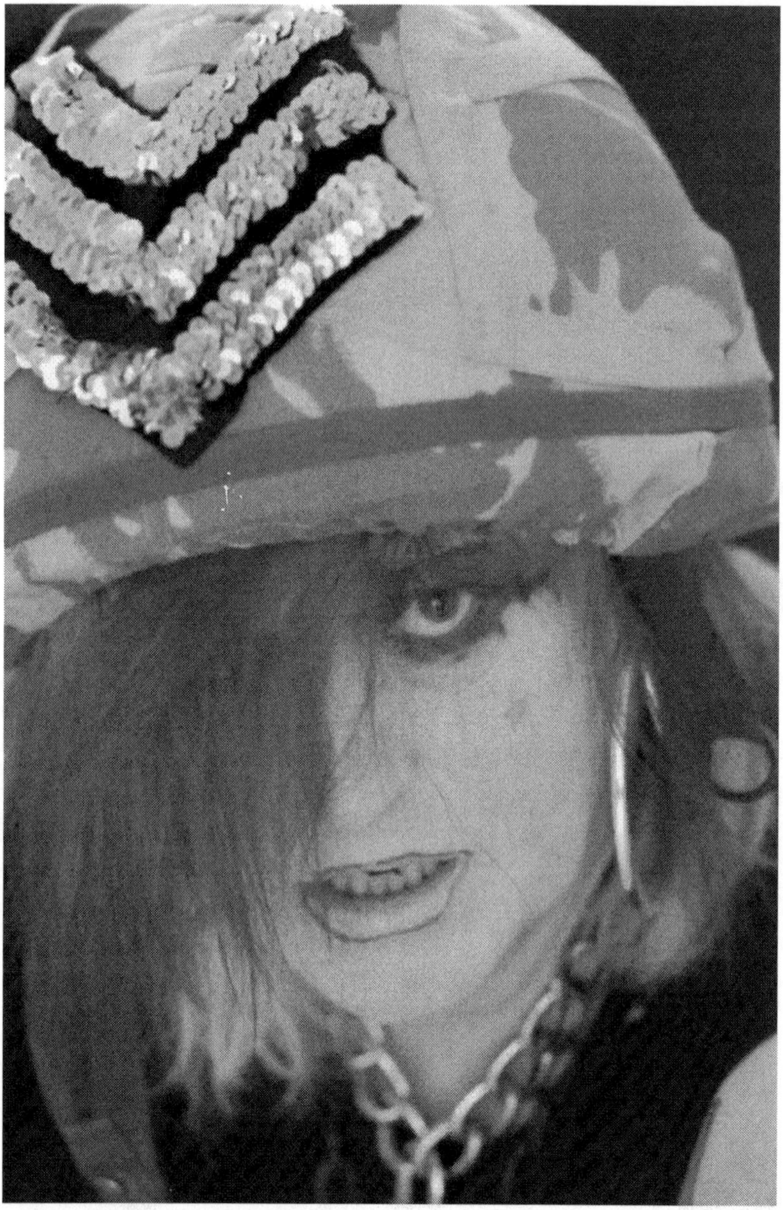

A SOLDIER'S PRAYER

From the sound of battles raging
To a lonely bugle call

Across the silence
Of the fallen
All alone

And on a little piece
Of no-man's land

A single flower grows
Amidst the silent pain
Of soldiers coming home

CAPTAIN SENSIBLE

Captain Sensible – a true pioneer of total skill and reality

I became very good friends with The Damned's Captain Sensible during the late 70's and early 80's. I watched him grow from strength to strength both in performance, with his keyboard and guitar work, and in his songwriting which, along with singer Dave Vanian is absolutely superb, and second to none.

I believe him to be the most underrated guitarist that this country has ever produced. Please take a little time to listen to his excellent work! He is so inventive and with a genius imagination.

UK SUBS (PART 4)

Sleeve notes from Endangered Species

When it was announced that top American superstar rockers Guns and Roses had recorded our song 'Down on the Farm' from our Endangered Species album I was truly elated and felt very proud. I can still see Charlie with his writing pad, jotting down the lyrics to Nicky's thunderous backing track.

This was only my second outing with the band yet we had achieved a new height in sheer energy and power and our confidence in the whole image of the band was taking a colossal shape of its own.

As we arrived at Jacob's Studios, Farnham, Surrey it felt and looked breathtaking... swimming pool, tennis court – and all in mid-summer the band was at its all-time greatest and dangerously unique best. And here we would all live whilst recording what would become 'Endangered Species.'

My first choice of song would be Alvin's 'The Living Dead' which he also sang. I watched through the glass as he performed it and realised I was in the presence of a true talent. I wish it had been a single, actually, but there you go!

Then 'Ambition' – I always have to play this masterpiece – not many may realise what a brilliant harmonica player Charlie is... on a par with Jagger, Dylan or even Rod Stewart, who all descended from Wardour Street's famous Marquee Club during the 60's when it was deemed the 'cool' instrument to play. Yes...

Charlie Harper was born out of a blues influence with a stage presence second to none.

Four great performers on this one great album. Every song was written on the spot, so to speak, and went down on the first take, capturing a terrific energy you could almost reach out and touch. With the incredibly high volume we worked with meant that Nicky Garrett was at his blistering greatest, like an unstoppable force of nature.

Please enjoy this very precious work of art and piece of punk rock history, knowing all the genuine rock and roll incidents and dramas which it contains! Just check out the almighty sounds of 'Lie Down and Die', 'Fear of Girls' and 'I Robot.'

Please also accept my sincere thanks and much punk love. And mostly to you the fans – you are all my friends who have stuck by us and believed enough that there might just be 'Life on Mars'.

Now, as Stevie ZeSuicide, I have two books available on Amazon, 'Rock and Roll Chronicles' and 'Fragile Butterfly' neither of which could have existed without your support and this fabulous sound you are about to hear once again – all songs produced by Nicky Garrett, of course. Enjoy!

www.steviezesuicide.com

PRELUDE TO AN OUTLAW

Modern day outlaw is a time when I had no-one to turn to. Alone and vulnerable I was lost to the world.

Now fighting back means so much to me, as I try to find myself once again. And again freedom from the curse of mankind's evil streak.

For those who turn their backs on shallow fear on order to keep on the right side of nowhere will turn on you like hungry lions to a lamb – yet they are no lions, believe me!

They are nothing but simple sheep and where lions are fabulous predators worthy of respect these shallow sheep will betray anything or anyone for popularity or wealth.

"Lions lose no sleep over the thoughts of sheep."

Stevie Ze

MODERN DAY OUTLAW

Alienation is now a part of my being

I have no middle ground left

Stevie Ze

Hotel bigotry, pub prejudice, restaurant refusals of service, were all part and parcel of my heady days of punk. Yet these incidents of being refused service or entry to somewhere are still at the forefront of my mind to this day.

Even now I don't dare enter a restaurant or hotel bar without fear of being turned away by some be-suited clot. When you are at a low I know how horribly debilitating it can be, and being despised or disliked on sight by so many was what put me so low in the first place.

What helped me was taking a good look around myself for somewhere a million light years away from all the trolls, the piss-takers, the put you down nasties and the fakes. A safe place, your own space where the prejudice-encrusted buffoons are not allowed to exist.

I eventually found it... in a love of animals, music and dress design. I hope to goodness that the decades to come will see much more understanding and respect towards the views of each individual. This planet belongs firstly to all the beautiful animals, the wondrous creatures of the sea, the insects, and hidden tribes who inhabit the world's rain forests – because they are all the true world of which, if God really does exist He created and planned for.

And as opposed to shallow twists to the Bible and other scriptures by Atheist nutters, or the one-sided, war-causing views of narcissistic hypocrites. There has got to be a peaceful solution outside what can only be described as a caveman mentality within our modern cosmopolitan world.

Having to witness people's dreadful behaviour towards fellow humans and animals, the barbaric things they say and do in the name of their particular religious or social views is, quite frankly, unforgiveable.

In other words, for all our sakes – live and let live. Have some respect and be good to each other! Gentle understanding towards different backgrounds is an almighty strength to possess.

I have been so lucky in my life to have witnessed the many international ways, customs and true beliefs of many sorts of cultures and people. Plus, so importantly, the most exciting foods from all over the world! This from my time in Singapore to all my touring in bands. I learned from my travels that to sit and eat together is such a positive and ancient tradition to uphold.

So – turn your back on doom and gloom and start a new dream of togetherness in food and drink, music and art, sports, and understanding.

"Music is the great healer, to create art without the interference of others is to create honest reality."

Stevie Ze

A friend of mine had a child at the same school as David Bowie's son, Zowie Bowie, when he was at his height with Ziggy Stardust. One day a limo rolled up and stopped outside the school. David himself stepped out, complete with orange hair, nail polish and outrageous attire, smoking a cool cigarette. My friend pointed over towards David and asked her son, "Do you know who that man is?" as the other parents stood aghast in the presence of the international superstar who stood by them. The child merely answered, "Yes, that's Zowie's daddy."

Making love with his ego, Ziggy sucked up into his mind like a leper Messiah. He came on so loaded, man, well hung with a snow white tan.

David Bowie

The innocence of our beautifully wondrous children is purely based on accurate assumption rather than the prejudice of appearance and prejudgement this should be a great lesson to us all!

"And if you ever have to go to school
Remember how they messed up this old fool
Don't pick fights with the bullies or the cads
'Cos I'm not much cop at punching other people's dads
And if your homework brings you down
Then we'll throw it on the fire
And take the car down town."

David Bowie

the one from out of space known as "Ziggy Stardust"
is discussed by Aliens, undercover of
Stevie ZeSuicide H.Q. ° Alien-isation
will always be my first love !!!
cc

BOOK OF QUOTES

"'time' is waiting in the wings, it speaks of senseless things, his script is you and me,... boys"
— David Bowie

"I'm a teen distortion, a survived abortion, a rebel from the waste down"
— Marilyn Manson

"for the loser now may be later to win"
— Bob Dylan

"I hope this doesn't come across as me, me, me !!! but I'm the only person I know, ... and even then, ... I'm not sure," ....
— Stevie Z

"If you have revolutionary potential, ... then you have a moral obligation to make the world a better place."
— Lady Gaga

"I want to be loved and accepted by all facets of society, and not be this loud mouthed, lunatic, poet, musician !!! but I cannot be what I'm not."
— John Lennon

"I'm Just a cosmic yob,
and Ziggy is my gift
to you,...."
— David Bowie

"Sticks and Stones
may break my bones
but names can be
fuckin' leathal,....
My guitar is now
an audible weapon."
— Stevie Z

"I never really hated
any one true God,..
but the God of
the people I hated"
— Marilyn Manson ©

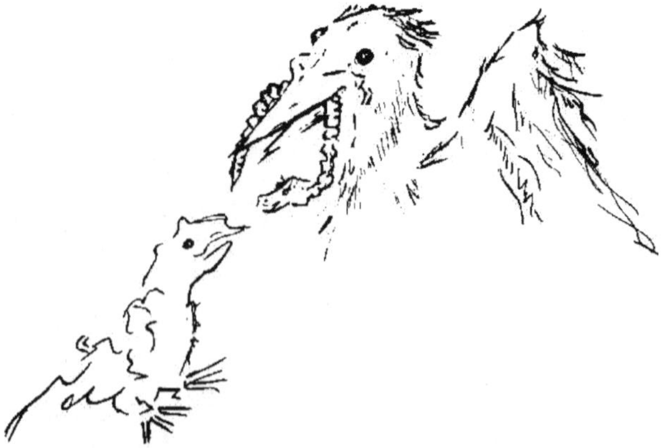

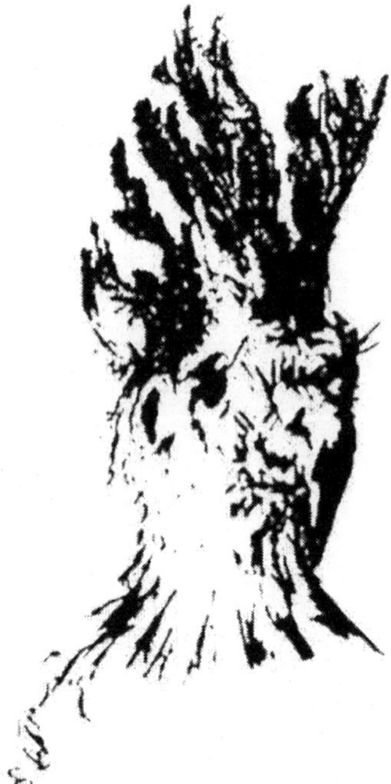

It can take a whole lifetime
to become as good as yourself
                    Miles Davis

A lot of what I've done is about
Alienation,....
about where you fit in society
                    David Bowie

Trust nothing but your own experience
                    David Bowie

I'm not a part of
the bland sublime,
because I don't wanna be.!!!
                    Stevie Ze

Being nailed into place
was never an option,
so off I went,
in search of a life.
                    Stevie Ze

don't pick the scabs,
or you will never heal
                    Marilyn Manson

segregation and isolation
are caused by human ignorance
toward difference
                    Stevie Ze

I never really hated
any one true God,
but the God of the people
I hated !!!!!
                Marilyn Manson

I smash up guitars
because I like them.
I usually smash a guitar
when it's at it's best !!!!!
                Pete Townsend

QUOTES

"You are how you look, people listen with their eyes."
— Versace

"Success is the greatest form of revenge!!"
— Frank Sinatra

"Be at one with yourself... for the body does what the mind tells it."
— Bruce Lee

The only creatures who are evolved enough to show pure love are dogs and infants. Not all treasure is silver or gold!!
— Johnny Depp

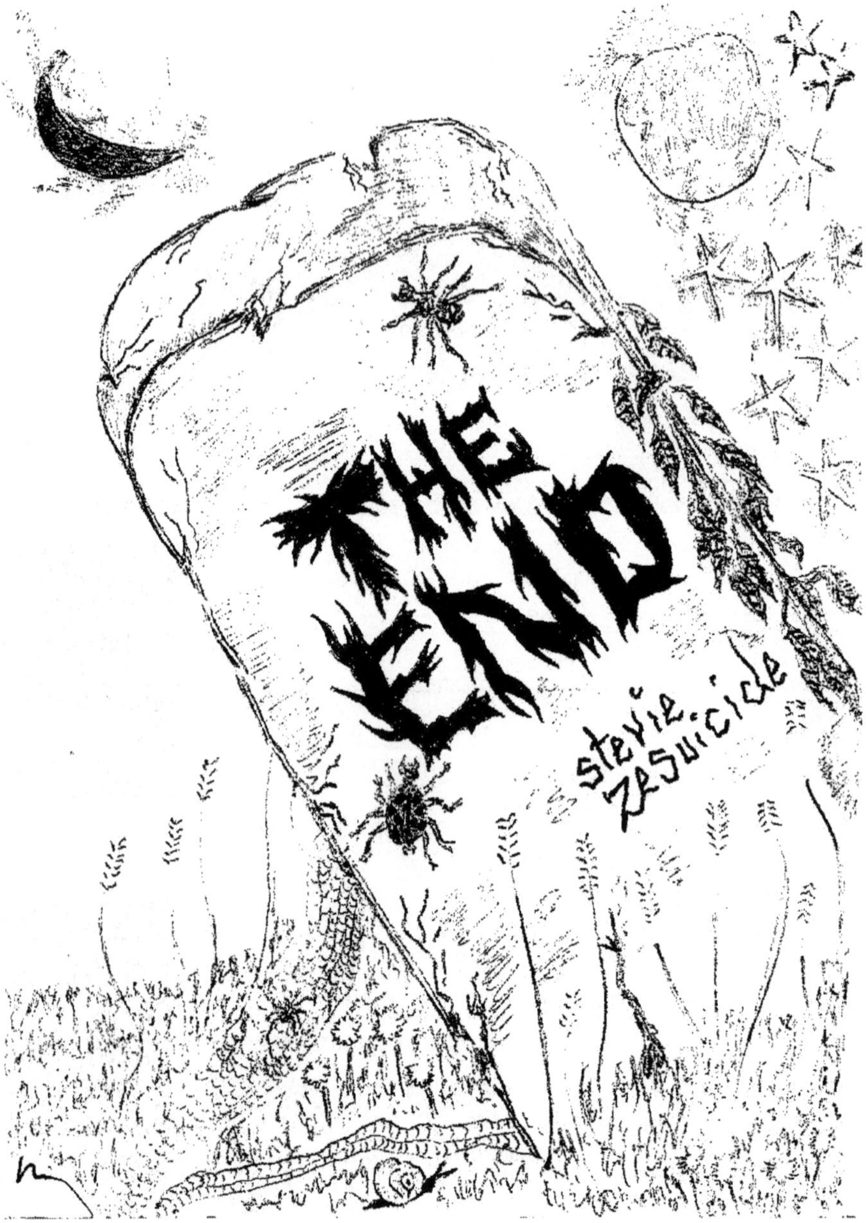
THE END
stevie zesuicide

SPECIAL THANKS

Mike and Terri Harris, for everything:-

Little London Records, TaM Management and TaM Entertainment

Beth Harris

for her voice on Bad Girls

Harvey Brewster

Photography

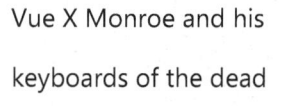

Vue X Monroe and his

keyboards of the dead

And to David John Earl: Guitarist, airbrush artist master, and his doggie Sydney

Stephen James Drury, 'Chutch', our former tour manager, now award winning top photographer

Also Lynn and Phil at MOR Music, York

Everyone at Digital Image, York – Steve, Ray, Theo, Nick and Ben – the greatest print team

Mike Laycock: Chief Reporter, The Press, York

To the best bloke of all time in rock 'n' Roll, punk and glam punk, Noizee Revolution devils – Dave Leaper, manager of Cyanide and Shed Seven… the man who was so affectionately called 'Dad' by our late, great lead singer Bob De Fries. You know Charlie Harper of UK Subs still refers to him as 'Our Dad' – the best sound man in the business to this day. A totally honest person and all-round good egg – all the punk bands so respect and love you.

My lovely friend John Wood and his doggies, Elle and Poppy for all his love of animals and creatures on this planet. A total punk and a person I can truly trust. Always love you John, and so will Becki, UK Subs, The Damned, The Exploited, and all the other bands you support and love to hear

And, of course, Charlie Harper, Nicky Garrett and Alvin Gibbs – I am so proud of all the work we did together, it was all great and I loved it so much

Rob and Carol Kimber in Cardiff, South Wales and all their family – such good people you can trust

Not forgetting – 'You're only as good as your hairdresser' – Lulu Monroe at The Salon Hair and Beauty Lounge, Gillygate, York with her lovely doggie, the fabulous Buddy. And, of course, her crack team: Racy Stacy Vancouver, the lovely, beautifully-formed, firm-bottomed diva that is Ben Superb who once sat Lady Gaga on his knee without too much trouser disturbance (or so he says, the naughty boy!), Kiki Kezza Kiaran the Kiwi, and sister Elisha Sherbet with their beautiful doggie, Dolby Dog Dalton, Mummzy Tricky Vicky Victoria – "What would my head do without you all?"

Let's all fight to end doom and gloom.

    "Commencing countdown, engines on

    Check ignition and may God's love be with you"

                                 David Bowie

    "Ride all night

    'Til the end of time

    'Til the black rain falls

    And the stars don't shine

    And the ice caps melt

    And the music's loud

    And the pavements crack

    Under red-hot clouds"

                             Stevie Ze

Printed in Poland
by Amazon Fulfillment
Poland Sp. z o.o., Wrocław